QUEST FOR POWER

Guidelines For Communicating The Gospel To Animists

by

Robert C. Blaschke

QUEST
POWER
FOR

Guidelines For Communicating The Gospel To Animists
Robert C. Blaschke

QUEST FOR POWER

Copyright © 2001, Robert C. Blaschke

ISBN: 1-55306-327-9

Cover Design, *Todd Baxter Design*
10027 Bora Bora Drive, Tega Cay, SC 29708

Typesetting and Layout, *International Graphics*
P.O. Box 38006 Charlotte, NC 28278

For more information or to order additional copies, contact:
Robert C. Blaschke
2135 Manawa Lane, Tega Cay, SC 29708 USA
(803) 548-3196
Email: bcbla@aol.com

Essence Publishing is a Christian Book Publisher dedicated to furthering the work of Christ through the written word. ***Guardian Books*** is an imprint of *Essence Publishing*. For more information, contact: 44 Moira Street West, Belleville, Ontario, Canada K8P 1S3.
Internet: www.essencegroup.com
Phone: 1-800-238-6376 Fax: (613) 962-3055
E-mail: info@essencegroup.com
Internet: www.essencegroup.com

Printed in Canada by
Guardian
B O O K S

COVER PICTURE EXPLANATIONS:

Front Cover
A Shaman dancing for the purpose of seeking empowerment from spirit beings.

Back Cover
The blood sacrifice of a bull on a grave for the purpose of sending the spirit of the deceased one to the "land of the ancestors."

I dedicate this to Carol Lee, who for forty-one years has been my faithful wife and companion, believing in me, encouraging me and all the while being a wonderful mother to our five children. We miss her for she is now with the Lord whom she lovingly served.

CONTENTS

Part I
Approach To Animists

Part II
Discipleship In The Animist's Context

Appendices

PREFACE

The purpose of this book is to provide Christians with guidelines for the communication of the gospel of Jesus Christ to animists in terms of their world view, culture and language. While animism is not solely an African problem, most of the illustrations are from the African context with appropriate illustrations from other cultures. For example, the research resultant from my several lengthy encounters with Quechua people (the descendants of the Incas) in Bolivia has confirmed to me that the animism practiced in Bolivia is conceptually identical with animism as practiced in Africa. Hence, several cases from the Quechua culture have been included.

While evangelism is the primary emphasis in Part I, Part II of the book provides a model developed for the training of church leaders according to the learning style of traditional African cultures where there is no resident Bible School. The implementation of this same simple format, I am sure, would serve well in other non-western cultures.

The intent throughout this document has been to be certain that the communication bridges suggested, both concepts and illustrations be culturally relevant, while remaining faithful to biblical truth.

My experience in overseas mission ministry has been with SIM under whose auspices it has been the marked privilege of my wife and five children to have lived and worked for twenty-seven years with the Boko people located in the isolated town of Segbana in northeastern Benin. It has been from within the context of this learning experience with God and the Bokos that the burden to write this book was born.

That the Boko Christian community of 1300 believers in twenty-five local churches is still growing, training their own evangelists and sending them to unreached villages is truly a tribute to the grace of God and His almighty power.

Spiritually, the Boko church has had a strong biblical foundation. While immorality has not been a prevalent problem, additional teaching on the power in the name of Jesus to do miracles and healing would be a witness of God's power to unbelievers, and give confidence to the believers in the area of spiritual warfare.

Nevertheless, a strong desire exists to evangelize their own people, such as their plan to send a choir and evangelists to a strong Boko animistic center in Nigeria for two weeks. They believe their efforts will result in many more being drawn from the kingdom of darkness to the kingdom of light.

The preparation of evangelists continues in two centers with as many as twenty at one of these Bible Schools. The promotion, the teaching and the financing of this schooling is completely self-generated as there have been no expatriate missionaries involved in the Boko ministry for a number of years.

One of the main prayer concerns is finances. While some of the local churches have been minimally supporting their pastor, a cash crop failure a few years running has deprived many self-supporting pastors and evangelists of funds with which to educate their children, support their family and continue in ministry.

Faith is strong in the Boko church. Leadership and believers remain faithful, trusting the Lord to provide the resources for daily life and ministry.

FOREWORD

The desire and quest for power is a universal human characteristic. Whether for personal gain or for personal deliverance and protection, it is found throughout the world. The author is well qualified to deal with this issue in depth.

Bob Blaschke was uniquely gifted by God to take the gospel to a primitive tribal area for which he later felt totally unprepared by his Western education. The personal discipline and single minded determination which he developed as a superb athlete (he excelled in football and baseball in college) stood him in good stead as an unmarried missionary entering an animistic tribe. He found that our Western manner of thought, which is logical and linear, was light years away from the thought patterns of animists. While his theological education had grounded him well in the Word of God, he was lost in trying to grasp the nuances of the thinking of a remote culture.

His greatest discovery was in realizing the difference between the Western and animistic understanding of salvation. We, in the West think of salvation as deliverance from personal sin. Blaschke discovered that the animist's concept is deliverance from an outside power or powers, usually evil powers, that dominate his life. That power is part of the created world in which we exist. To the Westerner, true worship is directed to the Creator. To the animist, true worship must be to the creation. The gods of nature (trees, rocks, animals, rivers, celestial bodies, even some human beings, etc.) become the object of worship rather than the Creator who produced these.

When Blaschke began to realize this enormous difference in belief systems, he was on the track to try to communicate the truths of God's Word to the animist. He found that they had no problem believing in the existence of God. He did not have to argue that point. Rather, he had to help them see that it is God Himself, rather than what God has created that must be the object of our worship. Because they were bound by fear of powers outside themselves, the first steps in salvation had to be for deliverance from those powers rather than from personal sins. This deliverance, of course, comes from the Creator. Only then could he deal with the issues of personal sins that so occupy Western approaches to the gospel.

The book is filled with graphic descriptions of how Blaschke grew in his understanding of the people to whom he wished to minister. He illustrates this with true, exciting and sometimes discouraging stories of what he learned. This is an eminently honest book. The author does not cover up the failures and disappointments. He speaks openly of those who turned away even after accepting the gospel. The reader will be caught up in the intense spiritual warfare that was being waged and the fact that victory was not always the outcome.

In the subtitle, the author calls this book, *Guidelines For*

Communicating The Gospel To Animists. This may lead many to feel it is not for them, as they are not missionaries to animists. However, quite the opposite is true. This book should be read by Christians in every culture, whether missionaries, pastors, teachers or lay people of every walk of life. We need to understand that well over half the world's population does not understand life in our Western way of thinking, that their understanding is diametrically opposite from ours. The universal body of Christ is composed of millions who come from such a concept and for whom spiritual warfare is a daily reality.

Also, the use of the word "Guidelines" shows the author's humility. He is not writing a "How to do it" book. He makes no pretense of having all the answers. Rather, he is sharing some lessons he has learned in nearly half a century of missionary work and thinking in the hopes that this may be of help to others.

Although I have prayed for my good friend, Bob Blaschke, ever since our days as college classmates over fifty years ago, I had no idea of some of the struggles for all those years. Now I am delighted to commend this outstanding book as being highly readable and valuable for Christians in all walks of life.

Dr. David M. Howard
Former International Director, World Evangelical
Fellowship
Former President, Latin American Mission

ACKNOWLEDGMENTS

There are many people who, in a variety of ways, have made their contribution without which this book could not have been written. I salute the many first generation Boko believers who, in the face of persecution and by their deep commitment of faith in their powerful new Lord, our Creator God, have challenged my faith and inspired me to record a part of their journey from darkness to light. My family, particularly my wife, then my four sons, Bob, Stephen, Philip and Joel, who believed that I had a 'story' to tell, persisted in keeping me accountable with the not so subtle question, "How far are you along in your book, Dad?" Then during a four month stay in Bolivia, missionaries, daughter Elizabeth and her perceptive husband, Hugo Vargas, provided Quechuan cultural insights and sound biblical perspectives which affirmed the veracity of the concept of spiritual warfare between Christianity and animism, not only in Africa, but in South America, as well.

I am grateful to Dr. David M. Howard, for graciously consenting to write the Foreword for this book. We were college classmates in the late forties. He understands spiritual warfare in the animistic context, having experienced it personally while serving as a missionary in Columbia. The Lord has used his gift of administration in prominent positions of Mission leadership. His passion for reaching a lost and dying world is evident in his speaking and in the several books and articles he has authored.

During the final stages of writing this book, Dr. Philip M. Steyne, professor of missions at Columbia Biblical Seminary and Graduate School of Missions, inspired me to persevere to the end.

By the contribution of their time and talents, Todd Baxter, Scott Sheppard and Gordon Moore, professional graphic artists, are much appreciated for the excellent job in preparing the document, the cover design and the visual aids for publication.

I cannot forget the Rev. Victor Musa, Nigerian churchman who informed me concerning traditional African customs. Then there was Pastor Primo, a lay Pastor in Sacaba, Bolivia, who graciously persevered with me through a series of Bible studies based on the basic concepts presented in this book. Dr. Larry Fehl, Jo-Ann Brant, Thelma Kephart and daughther-in-law, Charlene Hide Blaschke were of great assistance in the tedious task of proofreading the manuscript. Thank you to each one mentioned and those that I should have mentioned, for helping me make this project a reality.

INTRODUCTION

A PERSONAL HISTORY

In the beginning, I thought I knew quite a lot. In the end, I realized I knew very little. Albeit, during the intervening twenty-seven years of living in animistic societies, I did learn from these people and the scriptures with the Holy Spirit's guidance, ways to present the whole truth of God's plan of redemption in terms understandable to animists.

I had left home thinking, "My formal preparation for serving the Lord can't get much better than this." After all, I had graduated from a well known Christian college with a BA in anthropology and received an M.Div. degree from a quality seminary. I believed the intensive twelve week study in linguistics really set me up to tackle an unwritten language. Then, after a time of further study, I even earned a Masters of Linguistics degree with a minor in anthropology. I thought I was totally equipped to preach the gospel of Jesus Christ to those in spiritual darkness. Had I only known just how dark that darkness was, I probably would not have been so naive.

After a year of personal study of the Boko language in Segbana, Republic of Benin, West Africa, I had gained enough knowledge of the language that I could communicate about most of the basics of life. I had even learned enough Boko to begin sharing a simple gospel message. I felt pretty good about it until on one 'dark' day I discovered that the word I had been using to say, " *Believe* on the Lord Jesus." was, in fact, telling them to " *Doubt* about the Lord Jesus." Need I tell you how that made me feel?

As my knowledge of the language increased, I realized how pitifully little I knew of the Boko culture. The more I learned, the more I doubted the possibility of Bokos becoming Christians. For example, custom dictated that when a baby is born stomach down, that baby has an evil spirit. If allowed to live this baby, will one day rise up and kill all of the other children in the family. Therefore, for the sake of the other children, that baby is condemned to death. For the same reason the same penalty is meted out to the innocent baby whose top teeth come in before its bottom teeth. Fortunately, the Word of God from Isaiah 55:11 affirmed my calling and God's ability to save the lost; "so is My word that goes out from My mouth: it will not return to Me empty, but will accomplish what I desire and achieve the purpose for which I sent it." God's Word was able to bring Bokos to salvation.

My learning experience with God in communicating the gospel of Jesus Christ to the unreached Boko people group will help the reader better understand how God used scripture, the Boko culture and the experience of other servants of the Lord to help me offer to these people a relationship with the Creator God through a knowledge of Jesus Christ as Lord and Savior.

I, purposefully, have chosen to use the word 'guidelines' in the subtitle, because it is not my purpose to give the reader the impression that I have discovered 'the way' to win animists to Christ. Nor do I believe that scripture announces a universal, God-prescribed methodology that when used will guarantee results in winning animists to Christ. However, we can derive encouraging affirmation from two basic Pauline truths of evangelism found in Romans 10:13,14; 1) that the gospel must be preached and that; 2) "Everyone who calls on the name of the Lord will be saved." Interestingly, I have found that animists are open to hear God's word and have a felt need for deliverance. In addition to this, the ways of communicating the gospel are as limitless as God is infinite. If there are limits, it is because of man's lack of knowledge of who God is and/or his lack of faith in the power of God to act in accordance with His Word. When it comes to God accomplishing His purposes, Isaiah 55:8 reminds us, "…neither are your ways my ways…" Zechariah 4:6, also, recounts that it is "Not by might nor by power, but by my Spirit," that God operates in history. Then, the Lord Jesus Himself declares "No one can come to me unless the Father who sent me draws him…" (John 6:44). So, basically, God plays the major role in drawing men into a loving, saving relationship with Himself. His followers are merely the channels to convey the message of life in Jesus Christ.

Since God has chosen to use His followers to spread the message of salvation to unbelievers, it is the responsibility of Christ's followers to be continually abiding in Him, believing that without Jesus "…you can do nothing" (John 15:5), and that by the power of the Holy Spirit flowing through us, as Jesus said, we "...will do even greater things than these..." (John 14:12).

That this Holy Spirit power was present in the ministry of the early church believers is confirmed by the variety of evidences in the Acts of the Apostles. Therefore, I do not believe it to be coincidental that Paul, when addressing converts from paganism (animists), often used the term, 'power'. For example, "...the power of God to salvation..." (Rom. 1:16 NKJV); " Christ the power of God" (1 Cor. 1:18, 24); "...of the Spirit's power." (1 Cor. 2:4); "...in his mighty power" (Eph. 6:10); "His divine power has given us everything we need for life and godliness..." (2 Pet. 1:3). Paul, also realized that all things pertaining to the life of animists were under the power of Satan (Acts 26:18) and that only the power of Jesus' name could rescue them from "...the dominion of darkness..." into "...the kingdom of The Son he loves" (Col. 1:13).

COMMUNICATION

After having spent considerable time living in the animistic Boko society I had to adjust my perception of the definition of communication. The core of my theological training, while biblically sound, was monocultural in approach. We, the students were quite adequately equipped for ministry in the United States. The training was preparing us to be men of the pulpit. The key biblical phrase to reinforce this mind set throughout my three courses of homiletics was "Preach the Word..." (2 Tim. 4:2). "The world is your pulpit!" was another byword. As valuable as these courses were in preparation for public speaking, my experience in ministry in another culture taught me that a course in "Introduction To Listening 101" would have been invaluable. For without a knowledge of the Boko language and culture what could I have done with a 'pulpit'? During the first year after my arrival in Segbana, as well as many times after that, enforced listening was the order of the day while I studied this difficult, unwritten, tonal Boko language.

I learned in this setting that communication involves more than just the preacher, the speaker. There is also a receptor. Basic to any communication is a language or code mutually understood by both speaker and receptor. In military warfare mutually agreed upon codes for communication are established. Codes are used to keep the information secret from the enemy. Messages are encoded then sent to another military center, where they are decoded and read for a specific action to be taken. Without a knowledge of the code, the reception of the information would be in vain.

Other specialized communication personnel are also trained to intercept and decipher the enemy's encoded messages. When the enemy's code is broken, all of their strategy is understood and their inside information becomes available to be used in battle against them. Having prior knowledge of the enemy's information often determines the outcome of the battle.

Paul reminds us in his writings that we are in spiritual warfare with Satan and his hordes (Eph. 6:12). Therefore, it is imperative for the Christian messenger, first of all, to be knowledgeable of the work of evil spiritual forces. Then he must gain a working knowledge of the receptor's language. Finally, he must acquire as much information as possible about the world view and all cultural aspects of the target society to enable him to encode the gospel message in the code of the understanding of the people. The more receptor group cultural codes the speaker implements, the more easily will the receptors be able to decode (understand) the message. In anthropology these cultural codes are sometimes called cultural equivalents. Missiologists often call them 'redemptive analogies' or 'Points Of Contact With Animism,'[1] even the use of 'communication bridges' is valid. In other words, the messenger will look for cultural elements that are similar to biblical concepts which can serve to bridge the world view communication gap. The initial presentation of the gospel would begin with the receptor's concept followed by the introduction of the biblical concept. For example, there is a similarity between Christianity and animism in that they are both power religions. Christianity believes in the power of God. Animism believes in the power of spirit-beings. Knowing this, the missionary has abundant material in the Bible to speak to animists about the power of the Creator God and the power of Jesus. The powerful Creator God concept can function as a communication bridge (cultural code) into the animist's belief system which also believes in a Creator God. "According to the psychologist," Dr. Metzger confirms, "one learns by associating the new with the old, the strange with the familiar."[2]

Paul, one of the most successful communicators of the gospel, believed implicitly in the power of the gospel to salvation, but was, nevertheless, very sensitive to the culture, the beliefs and needs of those hearing the gospel. He understood the communication concept of listening, learning and speaking in the code of the understanding of his receptors. Our present day communication of the gospel would be more effectively received and understood, if we would adopt Paul's more balanced approach recorded in 1 Corinthians 9:20-22:

> To the Jews I became like a Jew, to win the Jews. To those under the law I became like one under the law… so as to win those under the law. I have become all things to all men so that by all possible means I might save some.

Or, as Paul's intent is here paraphrased in the same passage in *The Message*:

> But I entered their world and tried to experience things from their point of view, in my attempt to lead those I meet into a God-saved life.

Paul realized the importance of using the beliefs of the people as a bridge to communicating the gospel in terms of their understanding of life, their world view. A prime example is found in Acts 17:1-14, where Paul, a Jew, went into the synagogues in Thessalonica and Berea and "reasoned with them from the scriptures" (Old Testament). Yet in the same chapter, Acts 17:16-34, Paul as a teacher of a 'new doctrine' (according to the Athenians) presents his speech to the Areopagus in Athens. By first listening and observing their ideas and needs, he was able to bridge the communication gap into their world view by acknowledging their devotion to the 'Unknown God,' commend them for their sincerity, and then transpose their god-concepts into the truths of the true and living God. In this way, without attacking their beliefs and bad practices, Paul having earned a sympathetic hearing, used their beliefs as a springboard for a presentation of the gospel understandable to the hearers. And the response of some of the animistic Athenians was, "We will hear you again on this matter."

For the purposes of more effective gospel communication to non-Western societies, Western theological institutions would do well to incorporate basic communication concepts and Pauline methodology into their cross-cultural curriculums.[3]

WESTERN THEOLOGICAL APPROACH

As a part of the 'Western missionary force,' I have at times been dismayed that while we are very strong on preaching the theme of the gospel of 'salvation from sin,' we have been weak in presenting the gospel of 'power' to impact the practical daily dilemmas of animistic receptors. Surely, it is important for us to know that animists are in a daily struggle with evil spiritual powers who dominate their lives, yet from whom they must seek spiritual empowerment to deal with their dilemmas. Are we not aware that the dilemmas caused by these capricious spirits create anxiety in their worshipers? Evil spirits are involved in pregnancy, childbirth, sickness, curses, drought and death. Not only did my Western culture and theological training limit my understanding of life in the animist's spiritual realm, but sadly, some missionaries to animists are suspicious of power encounters or deliverance ministries. Mrs. Carolyn Butler, missionary to Zaire, assesses the Western missionaries' failure to meet the heart and spirit needs of animists as "A failure to recognize the reality of the spiritual world" and therefore, a

"Lack of expectation or even acceptance of a ready recourse to spiritual power." When this happens, she continues, "Even Christians have been forced to continue with or turn back to their traditional power sources."[4]

Why is it common practice for Western missionaries to emphasize in their preaching only the gospel theme of 'salvation from sin' (i.e. repentance from sin, lists of sins, sinfulness of man, man's need of salvation from sin, etc.) to all peoples regardless of their cultural beliefs and their world view? Could this not be a reflection of their theological training and culture? And since this sin theme is a vital part of the true gospel, the Holy Spirit, because He is God, continues to use it to convince men of their need for salvation, including animists. However, this theme, though biblical, usually escapes animists' understanding because it does not provide answers to the reality of the spiritual realm that he deals with on a daily basis (i.e. poverty, sickness, capricious evil spirits, community pressure, witch doctors, crop failure, etc.). It has been my experience that the initial approach for the presentation of the gospel to animists should first be the 'other part' of the gospel; the 'power of Jesus' that can provide answers to their dilemma of dealing with evil spiritual powers.

Another reason for the Western missionary's lack of answers to the animist's dilemma is that Western theology, has unintentionally, I believe, limited the definition of salvation to 'salvation from sin alone.' So that Romans 1:16a (NKJV) would read, "...the gospel of Christ, for it is the power of God to salvation *from sin alone*" [Italics is mine]. In other words, the definition and purpose of salvation in the missionary's mind focuses on the Western issue of sin and guilt, law and justice, a concept which, while biblical, does not exist in the animist view of life.

The sin concept has its roots in the Old Testament, where Israel, God's chosen people, was surrounded by animistic cultures. So, God gave His people the Mosaic law that they might know what sin is. Paul reminds early believers that "...through the law we become conscious of sin" (Rom. 3:20) and "...where there is no law there is no transgression" (Rom. 4:15). The Old Testament animists did not have that law. And so even today, the animist's typical response to the declaration that he is a sinner, is, "What is a sinner? What is sin?" With this limited view of salvation 'from sin alone' in his mind, the missionary tends to be less aware of the provisions of Jesus' power in the gospel to deliver the animist from the oppressive power of evil spirits. The Western approach seems to philosophize this way: "Get the sin problem taken care of and all the rest will fall in place."

There was a time early in my ministry that I was not aware that praying for a sick animist was, in the animist mind, a power encounter to see if Jesus' power was greater than the power of the evil spirits. For example, in a village where I had preached the gospel many times with considerable positive response, God was using a particular man to encourage the people to follow Jesus, even getting them to start building the walls for a church. Then this leader fell critically ill. In spite of my prayer for his healing ("Lord bless this man and if it be your will, heal him"), he subsequently died. It took me quite a while to

30

understand why the church building project there stopped and why I was met with a cool reception as I made further attempts to present the gospel. In fact, ever since that time, this village has been closed to the gospel. In the context of their world view, they determined that the power of the evil spirits involved in this man's sickness was stronger than the power of the Jesus whom I proclaimed. Had I known then as I know now, that this was as much about spiritual warfare, as it was physical healing, my prayer would have been a prayer of faith for Jesus' power to deliver this man from the evil forces that were binding him, both spiritually and physically. Neither my Western culture nor my theology had ever had to deal with the animist's power issue. Therefore, since the issue of spiritual warfare had never been addressed either in my experience or training, I went to Africa with a limited version of the gospel. However that may be, the burden of proof of the power of the gospel rests with the missionary to assure the animist that the reality of the power of God which Paul talks about in Ephesians 1:19b-21a, is available to them; "That power is like the working of his mighty strength, which He exerted in Christ when he raised him from the dead...far above all rule and authority, power and dominion." My experience concurs with Mrs. Butler's statement that "If we cannot show evidence of a spiritual power greater than the power demonstrated in animism there is little hope of making any headway for Christianity among these people."[5]

WESTERN VS. NON-WESTERN APPROACH

Expressing the process here in simple Western theological terms, one would say that Western evangelism presents the gospel of the forgiveness of sins, emphasizing first, the Saviorhood of Jesus. Then follows discipleship teaching on submission to the Lordship of Jesus. In the animistic context, having recognized the strength of the animist's belief and practice requiring submission to the authority and power of spiritual beings, evangelism amongst them should preferably first emphasize, submission to the Lordship of Jesus; the gospel of the power and authority to deliver and protect them from evil spiritual beings. Paul says in 2 Corinthians 4:5, "…preach…Jesus Christ as Lord…." Then, follow this with teaching on the Saviorhood of Jesus and the biblical concept of sin and forgiveness. Having been convinced by the Holy Spirit of Jesus' power, the animist is ready to take the step of faith to reject the authority of evil powers and submit himself to the protection of God's power and authority. This transaction of Lordship first followed by Saviorhood and forgiveness is described in Acts 26:18, "…to open their eyes and turn them from darkness to light, and from the power of Satan to God, so that they may receive forgiveness of sins." Because of the animist's world view, the preferred approach would be the presentation first of Jesus, the all powerful Lord, followed by Jesus, the loving Savior. To exclude either of these truths would be to introduce an incomplete gospel. An abridged statement of Paul's presentation of the gospel to the Corinthians, could be summarized this way:

> Preach the gospel—not with words of human wisdom, lest the cross of Christ be emptied of its power. For the message of the cross to us who are being saved is the power of God. We preach Christ crucified; Christ the power of God and the wisdom of God. My message and my preaching were a

demonstration of the Spirit's power so that your
faith might rest on God's power (1 Corinthians
1:17,18,23,24; 2:4,5).

To be sure, this so-called 'Western gospel', which I have
labeled 'salvation from sin alone,' while biblical, does not always
include the rest of the gospel (i.e., the Lordship of Jesus), which
is necessary to confront the evil spirit life experiences in non-
Western cultures. However, once animists are secure under
the umbrella of God's power, then their minds are open to
learn about the sin themes. As one African brother in Christ
confided in me, "Many Africans are born again, but not
delivered." They know of salvation from their sins and freedom
from guilt, but they have little or no teaching about the power
of Jesus that does protect them and is available to deliver them
from the power of evil spirits. This lack of knowledge leaves
them feeling vulnerable, so they walk through life with the
Bible in one hand and traditional religion in reserve, in the
other hand, just in case. This being true, then, if we do not tell
them how to overcome the evil spirits by the same power that
was available to Elijah and Paul, then we are just proposing
another religious option for them to use to manipulate the spiritual
powers for their own benefit.[6]

At this point, I began to think about the conceptual adjustments
that would be necessary to present the gospel to the animistic
Boko people in terms of their world view. In addition, since all
of the Boko Christians would be first generation believers, most
barely literate in their own language, and with very little of

God's Word translated into Boko, it would be beneficial to develop a discipling process corresponding to their traditional learning style.

The twofold challenge before me was clear: 1) present the gospel in terms of the animistic world view, and 2) disciple the new believers according to their traditional learning style, and still be biblically relevant.

INTRODUCTION - NOTES:

1.   See Appendix A.

2.   Metzger, Bruce M., *Lexical Aids For Students of New Testament Greek* (Princeton, NJ: Published by the Author. Distributed by the Theological Book Agency, 1983) p. vii.

3.   See Appendix D.

4.   Butler, Carolyn, "Applying God's Grace In An Animistic Society" in *Evangelical Missions Quarterly*, Vol. 29, Number 4, (Wheaton: October 1993) pp. 384-385.

5.   Ibid.

6.   Ibid.

PART I

APPROACH TO ANIMISTS

CHAPTER 1

STORY OF BABA

"No wonder we have no peace!" Baba blurted out with obvious anguish. As the light of this truth dawned upon him, he quickly inquired, "How, then, do we make a sacrifice to God?"

This gentle, bearded, gray-haired man, Baba, of the Boko tribe in Northeast Benin, lived in the isolated village of Belabelana in the subdistrict of Segbana. He had been responding to my presentation in the Boko manner of story telling, as I told the gospel story, beginning in Genesis. Baba along with his village people were hearing the gospel for the very first time.

A group of young Boko Christians, eager to bring the gospel of Christ to their own people, had accompanied me to this small village of mud-walled houses with thatch roofs situated under a cluster of some of the beautiful trees of Africa: the bread fruit tree, the locust bean tree, the kapok tree and the baobab tree.

The customary procession of greetings to each village household starting with the headman and his elders had already been completed. The Christians had found a shady clearing in the center of the hamlet at which to hold this open air gospel meeting. The hymns sung in both Boko words and music style told the gospel story. The crowd was quick to respond.

They had listened with interest when the young Christians spoke of the power of Jesus to deliver them from the power of the spirits. Then came my turn to proclaim the message.

My message given in Boko (however haltingly) started with mankind's dilemma; that man is in a daily struggle with spiritual forces, in a continuous series of power encounters throughout one's lifetime. This is a struggle to meet all of man's needs, and one in which all eventually lose. For the fear of death and it's inevitable victory, there was no solution. The power of spiritual forces always prevailed over the meager power of mankind.

Continuing, I told them of a time when mankind had everything in a perfect environment, an awesome paradise. Using Genesis chapters one and two, I described the Garden of Eden and the harmony between the Creator God and His creation. This place where amicable relationships existed between man and the Creator, man and his wife, man and animals and man with all of his environment that provided for man's total requirements: spiritual, physical, emotional, food, water, health, shelter, wealth and sexual. The intellectual and volitional needs were provided for when God made man in the moral likeness of Himself and made him ruler over all creation. God also provided for man's spiritual needs by creating him sinless, innocent, in communion with God and in a loving relationship with his wife.

Then proceeding into chapter three of Genesis, I recounted how man lost his peace (*Alafia*), by making one wrong decision: when Adam and Eve chose to reject God's instructions and authority and, by believing Satan's word, submitted to his authority. The consequences were that they lost the harmonious state of *Alafia*: the perfect environment, the perfect relationship between mankind and their Creator God and His creation. They exchanged the Creator's authority for the authority of Satan, the father of lies, and submitted to him and his agenda.

At this point in the story, I looked at Baba and asked if it was true that Bokos make sacrifices to things that God created, such as streams and rocks and the earth? He replied straight out that this was true. To make a point, I recounted an anecdote about a farmer visiting at the blacksmith's forge. While admiring the quality of a hoe, its shape, sharpness of the blade, the fine handle and thinking about all the work he could do with it, the farmer neglected to say, "Hello" and commend its maker, the blacksmith, for his good work. I then asked Baba, "Just how happy would the blacksmith be with that farmer?" Baba replied, "The blacksmith would be so upset that the farmer would get nothing from him." This by implication was the way Bokos have treated God: neglecting Him, yet worshiping His creation (Rom. 1:25).

Continuing the gospel presentation, I informed him that according to God's Word (holding up the Bible), God was very unhappy with Adam and Eve and reminded them of the penalty of death for disobeying Him. God's immediate judgment was to curse His creation. Man had to work to eat. Woman had pain in childbirth. The ground produced thorns and thistles. Animals were cursed: snakes were made to crawl on their belly. Death entered the world. Adam and Eve were banished from the paradise garden forever and alienated from God. They came under Satan's control, worshiping and serving him. This curse, this judgment which came about as the result of one man's offense has spread to all men. This offense is called sin, making all men sinners because all men have offended God by neglecting Him and worshiping not Him, but His creation instead.

"No wonder we don't have *Alafia*" was the anguished retort of this bearded old man when he realized that he and all his ancestors had been worshiping not the Creator, but rather objects that He had created and subsequently cursed (Gen. 3:14-19). The spirits to which the Bokos had been subject and worshiping for centuries were represented by the God-cursed creation in their culture (i.e., ground, rocks, rivers, etc.) When it dawned on Baba that he had elevated the God-cursed creation to a place above the Creator God, even to completely neglecting the Creator, the man was devastated.

Then I asked him, " Have you or any of your ancestors ever made a sacrifice to the Creator God who made and cursed the objects of your sacrifices and worship?" The truth of the implications of his total neglect of the Creator God and the accompanying consequences struck him like a bolt out of the blue and he replied again, " No wonder we have no *Alafia*." This was followed by a question that seemed to him to be the obvious solution to his dilemma: " How then do we make a sacrifice to God?" Baba had set the stage for the presentation of the good news of Jesus' power to deliver, to protect and provide for all of mankind's needs. This same powerful Jesus, was the one who made the one perfect sacrifice, the only ritual required to effect the restoration of mankind's *Alafia* and the broken relationship with the Creator God and His creation.

CHAPTER 2

STATE OF ANIMISTS

RELIGION

In the foregoing story the young Christians happily told about Jesus' power to deliver them from evil spirit-beings, that is to say, from their animistic religion. It is universally accepted that all peoples and cultures have a set of beliefs and practices that enable them to handle life's experiences that are beyond human control and give meaning to their lives. Steyne refines this definition when he says, "The animist defines religion as a system of beliefs, feelings and behavior which issue in rites, rituals and liturgies. By these he manipulates familiar spirit-beings to provide success, happiness and security in all of life."[1] This system of beliefs enables an animistic man to handle the daily dilemmas of life, which are controlled by forces more powerful than himself. It is through the practice of rites and rituals that the animist regains a sense of control and security that give meaning to his existence.

I began my message to the people of Belabelana reminding them of their dilemma: the Boko's daily struggle with spiritual forces. Their religion, as defined above, is Animism.

ANIMISM

The world renowned anthropologist, Sir Edward Tylor, states his definition of animism simply as, "The belief in spirit beings."[2] Dr. Steyne expands that definition to say, "Animists also believe that spirits inhabit certain rocks, trees, mountains, idols, shrines, geographical areas and persons, both alive and deceased, and that these spirits may be manipulated to serve man."[3] I would like to suggest that animism is the worship of spiritual powers who indiscriminately and unpredictably bring both good and evil to their followers, but whose ultimate purpose as described by Jesus is "...to steal and kill and to destroy" (John 10:10). That is why I believe the animist is set up to be a victim of his own system of beliefs. The spiritual world controls his environment. He is subject to the whim of capricious evil spirits under whose authority he exists, and from whom he must also seek empowerment to experience wholeness in this life. This puts animists into a life long quest with no certain assurance that they will be successful and no short or long term security during the search. I understand the animist's frustration with a system which promises wholeness in their lifetime, but never delivers consistently.

That is why a Boko Grandmother, whose name was Naa, was so upset when the pot of hot gravy she was carrying from the open fire slipped out of her hands and spilled uselessly on the ground. According to her belief system this waste did not happen because the pot was hot, or slippery or may have had a crack in it. The cause was spiritual, caused by someone's transgression against the spirits. A spiritual solution was required to restore order. She had to go immediately to the diviner to determine the reason for the loss and make the appropriate sacrifice or offering to placate the offended spirit. There would be no evening meal for that family. They would all go to bed hungry.

So, the animists who are convinced by the Holy Spirit of the greater power of Jesus, also believe that the gospel has the ability to meet their daily dilemmas. At this point, it makes sense for them to turn from one power system, that of the created spiritual beings, to the all powerful God of all creation for empowerment to cope with the exigencies of life.

ALAFIA

The order that Grandmother Naa was trying to restore in the life of her family is called in Boko, *Alafia*. This is a derived word, possibly from Arabic, used in several countries in West Africa and spelled differently by several language groups. I am going to use *Alafia* to identify the ultimate existence or ideal state of being for an animist. Steyne observes that the animist, "…strives for a world of balance and harmony."[4] Likewise, in the Boko culture and language, the concept of *Alafia* comprises this balance and harmony with all of creation, which when attained will issue in total peace and control over their own lives. The term *'shalom'* in the Hebrew culture and language is similar to *Alafia*.[5] Since the powers of the spiritual world are greater than man's, man must seek empowerment to exist and control the spirits which control his environment. Unless these capricious spirits change the 'rules' on him, "When the prescription *rites, rituals, liturgies, etc.* [italics mine] for the securing of power is performed correctly, power follows,"[6] the restoration of balance, harmony and wholeness, it is presumed, will occur. Unfortunately, the weak link in this system is man who "Must deal with the spirit powers correctly to produce success, happiness and security."[7] If one loses *Alafia*, for whatever reason, as this grandmother did, you can understand the fear driven urgency for the restoration of this wholeness.

SPIRITUAL POWERS

Why this fear of transgressing against the spiritual powers? Who are these spiritual powers with which the animist must battle on a daily basis? Are they good or evil or are they just morally neutral? What was their origin?

In his book, *"Angels,"* Billy Graham says, "The greatest catastrophe in the history of the universal creation was Lucifer's defiance of God and the consequent fall of perhaps one-third of the angels who joined him in his wickedness."[8] Paul understood this war of rebellion, when he referred to Satan, as "...the prince of the power of the air, the spirit who now works in the sons of disobedience" (Eph. 2:2 NKJV). This spiritual battle is further described by Paul as, "...not against flesh and blood, but against principalities, against powers, against the rulers of the darkness of this age, against spiritual hosts of wickedness in heavenly places" (Eph. 6:12 NKJV). These powers and spiritual forces are super human. By fear ("The moving power of animism"[9]), they hold man in subjection to their will.

Satan, a deceiver, "…masquerades as an angel of light…" (2 Cor. 11:14) doing everything in his power to "…Hold people captive and alienated from God."[10] He is cunning and clever, forever trying, "To discredit the truthfulness of God…And coaxing men to deny the authority of God."[11] "So God's forces of good and Satan's forces of evil have been engaged in a deadly conflict from the dawn of our history."[12] It is these same evil forces of Satan and the fallen angels, referred to by anthropologists as spiritual powers, that hold animists captive.

Animists today and those pagan cultures that surrounded God's people in Bible times have all been held captive by Satan's evil spiritual forces (i.e., Molech, Baal, Diana, etc.) and separated from God by their religious beliefs and practices. Yes, Satan has phenomenal power. But Jesus' followers, when endued by the Holy Spirit with the power with which God raised Jesus from the dead (Eph. 1:19,20), can "…demolish strongholds…" and "…arguments and every pretension that sets itself up against the knowledge of God" (2 Cor. 10:4,5), so that not even "…the gates of Hades will prevail against it" (Matt. 16:18 NKJV). This is "…the gospel of Christ for it is the power of God to salvation for everyone who believes" (Rom. 1:16 NKJV).

EMISSARIES OF SPIRITUAL POWERS

The emissaries of this system on earth are known by one of several names: witch doctor, fetish priest, diviner, spirit medium and shaman, among others. It is one of these that Grandmother Naa rushed to consult, since they are the interpreters of the source of problems and the prescribers of solutions to the spiritual imbalance. The diviner, in this case, became the mediator and manipulator of spiritual powers on behalf of Grandmother Naa.

When considering these spiritual powers, we would do well to define 'evil' as anything good or bad, which keeps mankind alienated from God and subject to Satan. Then we would not be surprised when Satan, the deceiver uses his power for his own purposes to produce either good, a pregnancy, for instance, or bad, such as a revengeful curse, and sickness even unto death. The evil one will do what needs to be done to keep his subjects dependent on him rather than on God. In Grandmother Naa's case, she had to know who was the cause of the spilled gravy and why. Did she offend an evil spirit or one of her ancestors? In any case, she would have to make the appropriate ritual prescribed by the diviner to placate the offended spirit. If she had been cursed by an enemy, the diviner must determine who it was and why so she can be empowered to protect herself and her family. In addition, if she can generate enough power through the right rituals, she can also cast a counter-curse on her enemy. The animist is primarily concerned with the 'who' and 'why' questions. Hence, her only recourse is to consult a diviner.

The Western humanistic-scientific response to the spilled gravy would have been, "What happened that the pot of gravy was spilled? Was the pot greasy and it slipped? Was the pot too hot to handle? Was the pot cracked and then broke? Did Grandmother Naa stumble? Did she run into someone or something?" After having discovered what happened, the Westerner must discover how to remedy the situation. That could be to provide a hot pad, remove a rock or stick, get another bowl and prepare more gravy so at least the family would not have to go to bed hungry.

If the messengers of the gospel are to bring "Deliverance to spirit-troubled people"[13] and "...see biblical Christianity practiced in animistic cultures, we must understand what we are up against."[14] We must also understand that in this spiritual warfare it is the name of Jesus, His power and authority alone that is our ultimate weapon to bring down these spiritual powers. The spiritual forces greatly feared by the Bokos are not omnipresent, but regional, manifesting themselves in seen, created things, such as trees, rocks, rivers, uninhabited areas (i.e., bush, jungles, mountains), earth, wind, animals, at cross-roads, leprechaun-like people, idols made with hands and personal enemies. Feared also are the unseen forces, such as sickness, death, ancestor spirits, evil spirits and curses. Is it any wonder that animists live in fear of such a formidable array of seen and unseen spiritual hosts of wickedness that Paul talks about in Ephesians 6:12. Animists are virtually powerless and at the mercy of these powers because they are alienated from the almighty power of the Creator God.

Being powerless in the face of the spiritual forces, man seeks to get control of his life through empowerment from these same spirits by manipulating and appeasing them. This search for power, if successful, enables man to survive, to protect himself from curses, evil omens, ancestor spirits and sickness. Also, by manipulating these spirits, man hopes to increase his powers of fertility, health, wealth, authority, respect and a good name.

If he gains enough favor, he can even persuade the same spirits to curse his enemies.

A government official from another tribal area, French educated, a Muslim by religion, assigned to a post in Segbana, told of his personal experience when he was cursed to die. Because of my life and involvement with animists over the years and our friendship, he felt that I was the only Westerner whom he could tell who would believe the account of witchcraft that he was about to divulge.

He was accused of having an affair with the local government nurse's wife. The nurse, he soon discovered, had conspired to curse him. The first indicator of this was the night he heard a hooting owl perched on his rooftop. The next day he fell sick and progressively got worse. That night, the increasingly heavy weight of pressure on his body was such that it became more and more difficult to breathe. Knowing that he was dying, he called his wives into his bedroom to distribute his various checkbooks and material goods. During his delirium, in a dream it was revealed to him who had cast this spell on him. These sorcerers he then revealed to his wives so that after his death they could be brought to justice.

With this knowledge, the wives went out of the house into the night, sounding out the death wail. My wife and I heard this while out for a walk getting a reprieve from the heat.

The curse consisted of the sorcerers locking a padlock with an evil omen in his name to 'lock' the curse on him. Then they proceeded to put an iron into a fire in his name. As the iron got hotter, the oppression and pressure on his body increased, making his breathing exceedingly more difficult. He thought that he would die from suffocation. At this point, he called for the sorcerers who had appeared in his dream to come to his house.

Shortly after his wives left, his chauffeur brought the sorcerers to his room where he told them he knew that they were the ones who had cast this curse on him. He informed them that his wives also knew and were prepared to take them to litigation after he died.

Seeing his physical state and hearing his threats, the sorceress, the chief perpetrator of this curse, also Satan's emissary, assured my friend that he would be all right. He would live and should not worry. With this she motioned to her accomplice and he snapped open the padlock, the sound of which all could hear. From that moment the pressure was released he said. He could breathe normally. His healing, which actually took a week, had begun. This is an example of Black magic, used by Satan's accomplices to control, enslave, destroy and keep mankind in bondage to his evil system.

Parrinder contends that:

> 'Black' magic is much feared, and many charms are worn with the object of defeating it by use of a stronger power. Babies are loaded with bracelets and charms to protect them from evil influences and witchcraft. Lovers protect themselves against their

rivals or jealous husbands. Farmers and blacksmiths arm themselves against accidents with their tools, which may have been caused by sorcerers.[15]

Westerners would tend to think that sorcery and witchcraft is practiced only by the illiterate and misinformed. But it is obvious that it is practiced by the educated and the informed, as well.

Because these practices are an abomination to the Lord, the Westerner's typical response would be to attack this sorcery as sin while exhorting the people to repent and refrain from it, using Deuteronomy 18:10,11, as back up:

> Let no one be found among you who sacrifices his son or daughter in the fire, who practices divination or sorcery, interprets omens, engages in witchcraft, or casts spells, or who consults the dead.

Then, by ceasing to practice this sin, supposedly spiritual warfare will also cease. Not so for the animist. The Westerner must realize that when the animist's faith in evil spirits is rejected, that faith must be replaced by faith in the power of Jesus to protect them from those same evil forces. Without Jesus' power, the animist is left defenseless and vulnerable to the retributive power of evil spiritual powers. His experience would be similar to Jesus' narrative where an evil spirit goes out of a man and then returns with seven other more wicked spirits making "…the final condition of that man…worse than the first" (Luke 11:24-26).

CONCEPT OF SIN

The Western missionary who begins his presentation of the gospel with the 'salvation from sin' theme will probably receive from his receptors either a blank look or a resentful expression. The 'sin against God' concept just does not exist in their world view.

Unquestionably, they know that God created the world. This is clear in their oral tradition.

Warneck puts it this way. To the animist, "God has become an abstraction, but they have personal contact with demons."[16] Paul says in Ephesians 2:2 that, they are walking according to the course of this world, according to the prince of the power of the air, the spirit who now works in the sons of disobedience. In their minds the Creator God created everything and then withdrew from man's world. Could this thinking have resulted from the 'original' animist's interpretation of the account of God banishing Adam and Eve from the Garden of Eden and the resultant alienation of God from man? If so, it follows that with the breakup of a God-man relationship, man would be released from any moral obligation to that former relationship. Man, by his own choice, alienated himself from God (Gen. 1:8) and "...turned to his own way" (Isa. 53:6).

With God, His law, and the 'sin against God' concept out of the animist's picture, "Tradition is the law for the animistic heathen. Sin is simply what offends the customs which all observe."[17] As Warneck continues, for the animist, "There are no moral standards."[18] That is to say that there is nothing similar to the Ten Commandments that obliges man in his relationship with God and/or man to conduct himself in obedience to that law. Make no mistake, animists who have never heard the gospel do have some inherent biblical, moral values (i.e., hospitality, no sex before marriage for girls, sharing material things, etc.). Their culture is not totally devoid of any good just because they are animists. However, "...there is no culpability or guilt in the Christian or Western sense, no sin as an offense against a lawgiver above and beyond life."[19]

Animists add another dimension to this. Since the offense is not against God, just tradition, one's behavior is only considered bad if one is caught or found out.

The animists, Warneck contends, "...have the idea of the permitted and the forbidden, but not that of good and evil." There is no sense of offending God and his moral code.[20] Boulaga explains further that "Every transgression conscious or not, is disorder and demands a restoration of order."[21] To return to that order, balance and harmony, which is the animist's state of *Alafia*, an animist must appeal to the spiritual world for empowerment through the practice of rites, ritual and liturgy to make this *Alafia* a reality in his world.

So, sin to the animist is transgression against his culture's customs and/or the requirements of the spiritual world. The Creator God is inconsequential to the animist's violations and/or the resolutions of life's problems.

The Western missionary who understands this concept would not be surprised at the animist's bewilderment when the doctrine of man's need for salvation from his sin is proclaimed.

An African evangelist related to me his frustration with his pagan parents' resistance to the gospel of salvation from sin. They could not understand how he could declare them sinners deserving of death when they had never killed anybody or stolen or been immoral. They had lived according to the code of their society's traditions and customs. How can they be considered sinners? What is sin? What does God have to do with all of this? This rejection of the gospel continued until he told them that they had offended the Creator God when they made sacrifices to God-cursed creation but never to Him (Rom. 1:25).

The biblical concepts of God, sin, death and salvation are foreign to their world view. Therefore, to start the gospel presentation with the salvation from sin theme just compounds the animist's confusion. Understanding their beliefs is just the beginning. Presenting the gospel of power is the next step.

CHAPTER 2 —NOTES:

1.   Steyne, Philip M., *Gods of Power*. (Columbia, SC: Impact International Foundation 1990) p.28. I owe a debt of gratitude to Dr. Steyne for many insights regarding the presentation of the Gospel to animists.

2.   Hiebert, Paul G., *Cultural Anthropology*. (Grand Rapids, MI 49506: Baker Book House, 1983) p.381.

3.   Steyne, 1990, p. 34.

4.   Ibid., p. 35.

5.   Long, Meredith, "Perspectives On Christian Health Care". *Centerline*, Vol. 20, No. 2. Billy Graham Center (Wheaton, IL. 60187, Spring/Summer 1997) p. 3.

6.   Steyne, 1990, p. 38.

7.   Steyne, 1990, p. 39.

8.   Graham, Billy, *Angels: "God's Secret Agents"*. (Doubleday & Company, Garden City, New York: 1975) p. 60.

9.   Warneck, John, *The Living Christ and Dying Heathenism*. (Grand Rapids, MI: Baker Book House, 1954) p.110.

10. Graham, 1975, p. 68.

11. Ibid.

12. Ibid., p. 64

13. Steyne, 1990, p. 15.

14. Ibid., p. 18.

15. Parrinder, Geoffrey, *African Traditional Religion. 3rd ed. (London: Sheldon Press, 1974 (ATR))* pp. 116-117.

16. Warneck, 1954, p. 110.

17. Ibid., p. 127.

18. Ibid., p. 126.

19. Boulaga, F. Eboussi, *Christianity Without Fetishes*. (Maryknoll, NY. 10545: Orbis Books, 1984) p. 81.

20. Warneck, 1954, p. 126.

21. Boulaga, 1984, p. 81.

CHAPTER 3

COMMUNICATION BRIDGES

MAN CREATED WITH POWER

When Baba compared his present miserable state to what I had communicated to him out of God's Paper (Bible) concerning man's original glorious created state, he became nearly disconsolate.

Could it be true that the almighty Creator God who had created man (man and woman) in the image of Himself (Gen. 1:27), holy and with the freedom of choice (Gen. 2:16,17), was not only powerful, but that He was also loving and concerned for man's welfare (Gen. 1:29; 2:15)? This thought revealed to Baba much about the Creator's benevolent character, which was so unlike the spiritual powers who had been dealing out mistreatment to him for a lifetime.

Baba could not understand why the powerful Creator, who had everything, wanted a relationship with man whom He had created, even coming to the garden to talk with him in the cool of the evening (Gen. 1:26; 3:8,9). He had tried to have a relationship with spiritual beings, but they were so capricious, how could they be trusted?

How was it that, without ritual manipulation, God generously gave man a position of supreme authority over all creation and then placed him in a paradise with total care, *Alafia*, forever (Gen. 1:26,28-30; 2:15,19,20; Ps. 8:5-8)?

And then perhaps the most pleasant provision God made for man was an innocent, pure helpmate, woman, whom he called, Eve (Gen. 2:21-25; 3:20). This was not the kind of wife that Baba knew.

This description of original man's perfect state of *Alafia* and of the Creator's character causes much introspection on the part of the animist. Not being a stranger to the supernatural, he is familiar with powers greater than himself. He desires a relationship with spiritual beings, but he is fearful of the evil they bring with them. He desires a relationship with the Creator-spirit, but how does that happen? Is it possible? Could this be the way to recapture *Alafia*?

The animists, Baba included, are mystified by the fact that man once lived in *Alafia* and had the choice to stay there, yet chose to go his own way, to go without God. Thereby, man by one act of disobedience lost it all (Gen. 3:23,24). Can you not now feel the distress, the anguish in Baba's statement, "No wonder we have no *Alafia*?"

To state clearly the contrast between *Alafia* and their present state of disharmony puts a longing for deliverance from oppressive evil powers in the already spiritually predisposed heart of the animist.

MAN WITHOUT POWER

To explain clearly man's loss of power, authority and *Alafia*, it is helpful to understand the biblical concept of original sin as it relates to the animist's dilemma.

ORIGINAL SIN

Man and woman were created innocent, but with the freedom of choice. God gave them the freedom to live in and rule over the paradise He had created for them (Gen. 2:8) and into which He put them. God made clear to Adam and Eve the one and only one restriction (taboo) He required of them was not to eat of the fruit of the tree of the knowledge of good and evil (Gen. 2:17; 3:3). Satan, the master deceiver, appealed to their pride and senses when he made the ambiguous, half true remark, "...your eyes will be opened and you will be like God..." (Gen. 3:5). In full knowledge of God's one taboo, they still chose to believe Satan's lie. "Their thinking became futile..." (Rom. 1:21). They thought they could "be like God" (Gen. 3:5), that is, "morally independent of God"[1] and in control of their own lives.

This defection of Adam and Eve and of all subsequent humanity, as well, is described in Isaiah 53:6, "We all, like sheep, have gone astray, each of us has turned to his own way ...." Their eyes were opened for sure, and they began to learn of the full implications of God's judgment: "...you will surely die," (Gen. 2:17) and of "...knowing good and evil" (Gen. 3:5). Oh, the sorrow and remorse they must have felt at that moment.

The taking of the forbidden fruit was the act of their sin of disobedience and rebellion against God's loving authority. Though they thought they would be like God, determining their own destiny, in reality they deliberately rejected God's authority and unwittingly delivered themselves into the hands of Satan, into his authority and control. Satan had trapped them and "...taken them captive to do his will" (2 Tim. 2:26). This was the most contemptuous affront they could have launched against the Creator God. If this is not so, then why did they hide from God (Gen. 3:8) and why did God break up His relationship with Adam and Eve by banishing them from the Garden of Eden (Gen. 3:23)? The account of the terrible consequences of their sin and God's curses on creation are found in Genesis 3:14-24. We are also told in Romans 1:18-32 about the moral degradation of man as he exchanged the authority and worship of the Creator for the worship of the God-cursed creation. By alienating man from God, Satan took control of man, bringing him unto submission to the power of his kingdom of darkness. That was the beginning of man without God struggling for control in the spiritual world, and of his ceaseless efforts to seek empowerment to manipulate the power of the spirits for his own purposes.

One of the most significant communication bridges into the animist's world view are God's curses on His creation. Animists have an experiential knowledge of curses. So let's look briefly at these 'original' curses.

GOD'S CURSES ON CREATION:

At the end of the sixth day of God's creative work, "God saw all that he had made and it was very good" (Gen. 1:31). Then in Chapter Two, the scriptures give us an overview of what that creation comprised (i.e., the heavens, the earth, the herbs, the streams, the animals, man, etc.). God created it so that all of creation was in a perfect state of balance, harmony and peace: *Alafia*.

When Paul wrote "...the creation itself will be liberated from it's bondage to decay..." (Rom. 8:21), it is possible that he was reflecting on Isaiah's prophetic glimpse into the future Messianic rule on this earth. This passage could also aptly describe the idyllic peace of the original creation.

> The wolf will live with the lamb, the leopard will lie down with the goat, the calf and the lion and the yearling together; and the little child will lead them. The cow will feed with the bear, their young will lie down together, and the lion will eat straw like the ox. The infant will play near the hole of the cobra, and the young child put his hand into the viper's nest. They will neither harm nor destroy on all my holy mountain, for the earth will be full of the knowledge of the Lord as the waters cover the sea (Isa. 11:6-9).

Some Bible scholars think that chronologically after God created the universe, God expelled Satan from heaven because of his attempted coup against the Almighty (Isa. 14:12-15). This is followed by his arrival on earth with his evil plans to continue his rebellion against God and His people. Adam and Eve fell victim to his crafty deception and thus changed the course of human history. God then proceeded to curse His good creation in the following order.

THE ANIMALS

After Eve took the forbidden fruit and gave it to Adam, they hid in the garden from God. He came looking for them knowing of their disobedience. Eve then blamed the serpent by saying to God, "The serpent deceived me and I ate" (Gen. 3:13). God turned to the serpent and said,

> "Because you have done this, you are cursed more than all cattle and more than every beast of the field; on your belly you shall go and you shall eat dust all the days of your life (Gen. 3:14 NKJV).

The snake at one time deemed one of the most beautiful of God's creatures was given this ignominious curse. Though verse fourteen above tells that all animals were cursed, the curse on the snake was greater, even to pronouncing the antagonism between people and snakes, which God declares in Genesis 3:15 NKJV:

> And I will put enmity between you and the woman, and between your seed and her Seed; He shall bruise your head and you shall bruise His heel.

The order, balance and harmony in creation was upset by this curse.

Bokos, as well as other animists, worship snakes. For example, the city of Ouidah on the coast of Benin is the center for the worship of the sacred royal python of the Fon people. The Fon driver of a vehicle would do everything possible to avoid running over a royal python crossing the road, even to taking the chance of running over people. That is how fearful they are of the power of the spirit-being in that snake.

There are ethnic groups in the Amazon River basin in South America who worship the anaconda. The Bokos and the Bariba's, also of Benin, worship the 'cousin' of the anaconda, the African rock python. This python is known to come into a village looking for food: a goat, chickens or a sheep. The people will do nothing to discourage, chase or kill it while it feeds. They will, of course, get out of its way and remove their children until it departs. They fear its physical presence, but they will not harm it because of its spirit-being powers. Bokos respond to this deadly serpent with kindly words of encouragement, "Eat slowly, slowly," they tell it as it consumes one of their sheep. Out of fear, they worship it for its spiritual powers. Their minds are darkened, not knowing that they worship a God-cursed creature.

WOMAN

Because of her disobedience, God said to Eve,

> I will greatly multiply your sorrow and your conception: in pain you shall bring forth children; your desire shall be for your husband, and he shall rule over you (Gen. 3:16 NKJV).

Who can deny the reality of this curse? Is there a society in this world or even one woman who does not suffer discomfort during pregnancy and childbirth? For some, it brings even death.

When Eve sinned, Satan exploited this curse to hold women in bondage to his spiritual beings in the area of women's fertility by insisting that he had the power to give them a pregnancy. For instance, a Boko couple will often go together to make a sacrifice, usually a chicken, at the location of the spirit who 'gives' pregnancies. If, as a result, the wife conceives, the couple is forever beholden to that spirit to make occasional visits to present a thank offering. They will also name the child after that spirit, such as Wolu Waa. Wolu is the name given to every first-born male child and Waa is the name of the river spirit. Everyone will always know that a child whose name includes, Waa, is the gift of the spirit-being which inhabits the river called Waa.

Because of the risks involved in childbirth and the accompanying pain, the Boko women bring all the fetishes in the village made to represent a dead twin, to the 'delivery' hut to invoke the power of these spirits to assure a safe delivery. After the safe birth, the couple must revisit the river to bring a thank offering for this child. This is another ploy of Satan to keep animists in bondage to him and alienated from the Creator, the true giver of life.

As if this was not enough trouble for woman, her place as a suitable helper to her husband (Gen. 2:18) was changed to that of being subject to her husband (Gen. 3:16). Notes in the NIV Study Bible describe woman's new position as designed around 'desire' and 'rule.' "Her sexual attraction for the man, and his headship over her, will become intimate aspects of her life in which she experiences trouble and anguish rather than unalloyed joy and blessing."[2]

This is clearly illustrated, even today in cultures not impacted by the love of Christ where one finds that women are held in a very low place in society. For instance, in Muslim societies it is not uncommon for women, once they are married to never be permitted to go beyond the walls of their house. If they do leave, they must always be accompanied by a member of the family.

In my travels, I have personally heard women referred to as 'beasts of burden.' One can believe this to be true when one sees a woman as we did in Bolivia, on her way home one evening with her young son who was carrying a plastic bag full of food and his mother's shoes. We were aghast at her loads as we stopped to greet her as she paused for a brief rest. She not only was carrying large plastic bags loaded with vegetables in each hand, but on her back in her shawl she was carrying about 75 lbs. of potatoes, plus some other vegetables. She was also nine months pregnant. Many times African women walk with tremendous loads which take two other people to lift onto their head. When one considers the work laid on them, the saying "A woman's work is never done" becomes an understatement in these societies.

This judgment on women in the Garden of Eden that day was severe and continues to be severely enforced by men in some areas of the world.

THE GROUND

God originally designed ground to produce food. It was His gift to mankind for his daily nourishment. While man was made responsible to care for this garden, the only effort he had to put forth to maintain his strength was to glean and eat.

> And God said, "See, I have given you every herb that yields seed which is on the face of the earth, and every tree whose fruit yields seed; to you it shall be for food. The Lord God planted a garden eastward in Eden and there He put the man whom He had formed. And out of the ground the Lord God made every tree grow that is pleasant to the sight and good for food. The tree of life was also in the midst of the garden and the tree of the knowledge of good and evil. Then the Lord God took the man and put him in the garden to tend and keep it (Gen. 1:29; 2:8,9,15 NKJV).

How easy it was for man to find and eat nourishing food. They even could have eaten the fruit of the tree of life which would have guaranteed them life forever (Gen. 3:22). Adam and Eve were truly blest. To have forsaken all of this, while having full knowledge of the penalty for disobedience, indicates that their drive to control their own destiny must have been very strong. But then again, let's not forget that Eve was deceived by Satan, as well.

It would be interesting to know what was going on in Adam's mind when God pronounced the curse on the ground by saying, "Cursed is the ground for your sake…. Both thorns and thistles it shall bring forth" (Gen. 3:17a, 18a NKJV). Before this time, Adam just had to tend the garden. Now he had to work it and work very hard to survive.

Man has always been and always will be dependent on the soil for the source of his food. But with the soil now cursed God added thorns, thistles and weeds to the good things produced.

Having rejected God's Word, mankind was now tuned into and subject to Satan's directives and control, even to sacrificing to the spirit of the ground to hopefully assure him a good crop and plenty to eat. Many are the animistic societies that have made the ground one of their gods. For the Bokos, making yam hills begins near the end of the calendar year. At this time, only the patriarch or the oldest able bodied male member of the family makes the trek out to the family farm all by himself to perform the ceremony of making the first three yam hills; the first being the largest of them all. On this first hill, he will sprinkle the blood of a chicken sacrificed right there to the spirit-being inhabiting the soil. Knowing that this blood ritual is required by the spirit, the farmer is hopeful but never certain that the spirit will thus be compelled to produce a good crop of yams. At harvest time, then, a thank offering must first be presented to the earth spirit before anybody is permitted to eat the first new yams.

The Quechuas and Aymaras in Bolivia perform a ritual similar to the Bokos when they bury a llama fetus in their farm soil to placate *Pachamama*, the Mother Earth, as they beseech her to bless them with a good crop. They believe that "*Pachamama* renders all natural elements, such as the sun, earth, people, animals, wind and water…it is the representation of all the earth's energy. It gives vitality, force and union."[3]

One of the most hideous of spirits of the God-cursed ground produced by Satan to hold people in bondage out of fear of death is *El Tio*, the devil of the mines in Potosi, Bolivia. The miners worship this one who is a

> …rapacious deity with the clothes of a miner and the beard of a Spaniard. Several times a year, they sacrifice llamas to this being, adorning the mouth of the mine with blood, so that he will not eat them. At Carnival time, the miners dance to the devils tune…dressed as Spanish lords, African slaves and the devil. The Devil, or Tio, is a potent symbol of the miner's life…and the center of their religious life. This devil…has tremendous horns, around one of which is coiled a snake, a Quechuan symbol of good luck. The miners, who offer him cigarettes, cocoa leaf and his preferred drink of grain alcohol, like to call him *viciado*, full of vices. He enjoys being insulted, so at times they cuss him out. He is at once comrade and lord, protector and destroyer of the mines.[4]

The pouring out of libations also demonstrates man's fear of the spiritual powers of the ground. A libation is the pouring out on the ground of one's alcoholic drink out of reverence to and in hopes of engendering the good favor of the earth god. Amongst the Quechua, the drink would be poured out to *Pachamama*.

All of these practices represent the ultimate expression of Satan's degenerate character and his vile plan to keep men captive and alienated from the loving benevolent Creator God. Satan capitalized on God's curse on the ground by developing it further into an abominable system of transgressions against the Creator God, all of which add to the misery and destruction of mankind.

THE MAN

As the ground was cursed, so was man. "In toil you shall eat of it, *the cursed ground* [italics mine] all the days of your life. In the sweat of your face you shall eat bread"(Gen. 3:17b, 19a NKJV). From a program of gleaning food to thrive, Adam went to forced labor to survive. "Therefore the Lord God sent him out of the garden of Eden to till the ground from which he was taken" (Gen. 3:23 NKJV).

For Adam to survive he not only had to contend with hard, weed-filled soil out in the boiling sun, but he had to manufacture his own soil cultivating tools. Here again, Satan extended his oppressive system of ritual ceremonies and liturgy required for man to gain empowerment from not only the spirit of mother earth, but from the tools used to till mother earth. One day while visiting in a village, I came upon a witch doctor as he was slitting the mouth of a baby chick between its beaks. Then, to the accompaniment of a liturgical chant, he dripped the chick's blood a drop at a time on a devotee's hoe and bow and arrow. Fearful lest his own power and that of his hoe and bow and arrow be insufficient, the farmer sought spiritual empowerment, specifically for the labor on the farm and for success on the hunt.

Satan's authority and his word, resulting from Adam and Eve's one act of disobedience, still extends to all aspects of the animist's life. He is powerless to disassociate himself from the spirits' involvement and power.

However, the ultimate humiliation for Adam, even greater than having to work for his food, was to have experienced and then lost his God-delegated sovereignty and power as the ruler over all of God's creation. The Psalmist affirms the divine benediction of this high and lofty place of honor of bearing the image of the Creator and of governing His creation.

> For you have made him a little lower than the angels.
> And you have crowned him with glory and honor.
> You have made him to have dominion over the works
> of Your hands; You have put all things under his
> feet. All sheep and oxen—even the beasts of the
> field, the birds of the air and the fish of the sea that
> pass through the paths of the seas (Ps. 8:5-8 NKJV).

Rather than choosing to live in harmony and peace in the blissful state of unity with God and as stewards of His creation forever, Adam and Eve chose to believe Satan's lie that "…you will be like God" (Gen. 3:5 NKJV). Consequently, God's curse and His judgment cut right to the heart of man's pride and rebellion, depriving him of what he wanted most: power to determine his own destiny. Tragically, Adam and Eve's misplaced faith in the great deceiver's lie moved them into the servitude of Satan's kingdom of darkness and alienated from God.

LIFE

God's penalty for disobedience, "...for when you eat of it (the tree of the knowledge of good and evil) you will surely die" (Gen. 2:17; 3:3), began to unfold before their very eyes. While it is true that they did not immediately die physically, they realized at once that they were naked. Being no longer innocent, they were ashamed and tried to clothe themselves, however inadequately, with leaves. Then full of shame, they hid from the Lord God among the trees of the garden (Gen. 3:7,8).

When God proceeded to announce the curses and judgments on His creation, Adam and Eve suddenly realized that the reward for disobedience promised by Satan was quite different from the penalty promised by God.

God then deprived them of eternal life by banishing them from the garden, "...lest he put out his hand and take also of the tree of life, and eat and live forever — therefore the Lord God sent them out of the garden of Eden" (Gen. 3:22,23 NKJV). Then "...He placed a cherubim at the east of the garden, and a flaming sword which turned every way, to guard the way to the tree of life" (Gen. 3:24). Having already heard from God that they were dust and would return to dust, they knew for sure that they would die. With this final step to bar them from the garden and the tree of life, they knew that their inevitable destiny of alienation from God, powerless and subject to Satan's authority, was assured. Disobeying God always terminates in death. For Adam and Eve it seemed more like multiple deaths when one compares all that they had with all that they had lost. Life was cursed. Death entered the world. Paul expressed it this way: "...by the trespass of one man, death reigned (Rom. 5:17)...in this way death came to all men, because all have sinned" (Rom. 5:12). Paul confirms that it is the devil, "...who holds the power of death" (Heb. 2:14).

No wonder animists fear death and fear the power of spirit beings; Satan holds the fear of death over animists bringing them into submission with the threat of all possible kinds of misfortune (Heb. 2:14 NKJV). These threats from the offended spirits are for acts of omission or commission, which due to the evil spirit's fickleness cannot always be predetermined by the worshiper.

Each culture has its own way to handle death and its accompanying complications. The Bokos believe that at death the spirit of the deceased stays around the family household to harass and harangue the living members of the family. Not until the appropriate rites and liturgy are performed will the spirit of the deceased be pleased to move on to the resting place of the ancestors.

One of the rituals that must be carried out by the Bokos during the funeral ceremony is the spilling of blood on the grave of the deceased. The wealth of the family, the social position and the power of the dead one will determine how many animals (sheep, goats, chickens and bulls) will be slain. Once I came late to the funeral of an important person to find the blood already spilt not just on the grave, but over the ground adjacent to the grave that covered an area approximately 26 ft. x 26 ft. (8m x 8m). Does this not indicate fear of death, fear of the spirit of the deceased and fear of the one, Satan, who holds the power of death? The breath of eternal life which God breathed into man had started out so perfectly, but abruptly became the curse of death, a judgment which subsequently passed to all men.

RELATIONSHIPS

Some goal-oriented people in Western societies will sacrifice relationships in order to succeed. Whereas, people in non-Western societies will sacrifice work goals to maintain relationships. So, when members of these societies observe the same incident or hear the same story, the difference in their responses is determined by their world view.

In the story of Abraham and Lot (Gen. 13 & 19), Abraham gave Lot the first choice of land in which to settle his family. Lot chose the best, the fertile land, which also included the immoral city of Sodom. This choice eventually destroyed his family. A Westerner's response to this incident would be, "The moral of the story is this, because Lot chose riches he reaped the harvest of greed." A non-Westerner might say, "The moral of the story is, if a man shows disrespect for his elders, he will destroy his own family" (from Jacob Loewen, source unknown).

Or consider the Western response to the cause of a highway automobile accident. Either carelessness on the part of the chauffeur or the mechanical failure of the vehicle would usually be judged to be the cause. The response of the non-Westerner (the animist) would be that a curse had been put on one of the passengers. A diviner, therefore, would have to be consulted to determine who did this and why. Then the appropriate ritual would be performed to restore the relationship with the offended spiritual beings that instigated the accident. The key to the restoration of balance and harmony in the animist's world is always performance of the correctly and meticulously prescribed ritual.

Unfortunately, I had to learn the hard way about the high value attached to relationships in animistic societies. I recall the building of a growing friendship with a Muslim teacher. We enjoyed discussing many topics, including our respective religions. As it turned out, in my zeal to herald the truth, I "pushed him into a corner" philosophically, which left him embarrassed with no way out. I had won the argument, proclaimed the gospel, but lost a relationship. If I had the opportunity to do it over again, I would seek godly wisdom to "be wise as serpents and harmless as doves" (Matt. 10:16 NKJV).

One conclusion that be can drawn here is that the Westerner focuses on precepts and empirical evidence, while the non-Westerner focuses on relationships and spiritual reality. This is a concept very difficult for the Westerner to accept and implement because of our zeal to preach the gospel of salvation from sin to lost souls. Hence, the importance of relationships can get overlooked or just accorded a lesser priority.

Now back to the curse on relationships and how that one act of rebellion changed Adam and Eve's relationship with the Creator and His creation.

Man, as he was created, was the crown and glory of God's creation and the ruler over it all (Gen. 1:26). But God banished this fallen man and his wife from that pleasant and wonderful garden over which he had total dominion under God. Adam also had a ruler-subject relationship with the animals, whom God brought peaceably to him to name (Gen. 2:19,20). And it is presumed that even the harmony which existed then between animals was spoiled, not to be restored until the kingdom age when once again "...the wolf will live with the lamb" (Isa.11:6-9).

Eve's relationship with Adam, her husband, deteriorated from that of being a 'suitable helper' to having a husband who "...will rule over you" (Gen. 3:16). By believing Satan's lie that she could be like God, controlling her own destiny, she was reduced to a position of subjection to her husband. That is not what she had in mind. Even today, women, in general struggle with that 'lowly' position.

Can you even imagine just how disastrous the breakup of God's relationship with man must have been when God banished Adam and Eve from the Garden of Eden (Gen. 3:23,24) lest they "...take also of the tree of life, and eat, and live forever" (Gen. 3:22)? They were alienated from God, without His fellowship, without His protection, powerless and subject to the one whose word they accepted as truth, Satan. "They exchanged the truth of God for a lie, and worshiped and served created things rather than the Creator" (Rom. 1:25). This resulted in the weakened moral and spiritual state of fallen man, susceptible to the wiles of the devil's schemes. This is the daily dilemma of the animist.

So man without a relationship with God, living in the kingdom of darkness, began to walk "…according to the prince of the power of the air, the spirit who now works in the sons of disobedience" (Eph. 2:2 NKJV).

It was through the one trespass of rejecting God's authority in their lives, that "…sin entered the world through one man, and death through sin" (Rom. 5:12). And so it happened just as God said it would: "…for in the day you eat of it you shall surely die" (Gen. 2:17 NKJV).

Man today is in desperate need of the power of the gospel to deliver him from the kingdom of darkness to the kingdom of God, from Satan's authority to God's authority, from alienation from God to allegiance to God through repentance and the forgiveness of his sin. To achieve the restoration of all these broken relationships, mankind needs a ritual far greater and more powerful than any ritual Satan and his demons are capable of providing or that mankind can invoke. Only the Creator God can effect such a powerful ritual.

CHAPTER 3 —NOTES:

1. The Holy Bible, *New International Version*. Copyright 1973, 1978, 1984 by International Bible Society. NIV Study Bible. p.9

2. Ibid., p.9.

3. *The Bolivian Times*, "One People, One Earth", by Christele Jaime, Thursday, February 10, 2000, Vol. VIII, No. 6, p. 8.

4. *The Bolivian Times*, "Potosi: the Mountain That Eats Men", pp 8,9. Thursday, January 6, 2000, Vol. VIII No. 1. from *I Am Rich Potosi: The Mountain That Eats Men* by Stephen Berry, copyright 1999, The Monacelli Press, p.9.

CHAPTER 4

GOSPEL COMMUNICATION IN CONTEXT

PREPARATION

THE ANIMIST'S DILEMMA

To put the gospel presentation in context, we would first do well to recall the animist's dilemma. Animists are in a daily struggle with spirit beings. By the use of rites, rituals and liturgies, animists cajole, appease, placate and manipulate these spirit forces for empowerment to try to gain control of all aspects of their daily lives.

Being subject to these capricious and fickle evil spirits, animists can only hope that the spirits will look favorably on their efforts and grant their favors.

The animistic world view has it roots in Adam and Eve's sin of rebellion against God's authority and power which they rejected when they "…exchanged the truth of God for the lie, and worshiped and served the creature rather than the Creator." (Rom. 1:25). We need to recognize that, "The devil is the personification and the instigator of the power opposed to God; it was he who deceived our forefathers and persuaded them to idolatry."[1] Hence, they moved from God's kingdom into the kingdom of the spirit world of the creature, Satan, where his power and authority dominates the animists world view and thus everything in their daily lives. They understand supernatural evil power. They live by it. They are controlled by it. They die by it. Paul correctly perceived that Satan, "The god of this age has blinded the minds of unbelievers, so that they cannot see the light of the gospel of the glory of Christ" (2 Cor. 4:4).

They need a greater power to free them; to move them back into God's power and authority. How can this happen?

COMMUNICATION BRIDGES

To summarize Paul's model which was discussed earlier; learn the culture, the beliefs, and the needs of those to whom you will be presenting the gospel. Missiologist and Professor Dr. Alan Tippett quotes an appropriate statement by Henri Maurier who said, "It is not enough for the apostle to learn what God has said; he also has to understand the men to whom he is bringing the Word."[2] This involves a lot of 'down time' from preaching which must then be dedicated to listening. The more zealous missionary may feel sitting around and listening to be a waste of time without realizing that the real essence of the missionary's ministry is his life and the love of Jesus seen in him. This is his most powerful message. Listening, also lets people know just how important they are. As Warneke puts it, "The understanding of God's love rises in the heathen heart when he sees the unselfish love of the messenger who seeks not his own."[3]

As Paul took into account biblically-relevant customs of the people, so the missionary should form a data base of dynamic cultural equivalents starting, for example with those related to God's curses on creation as previously recounted. Add to this other communication bridges or redemptive analogies discovered in your study of the local culture. For example:

- the Boko concept of forgiveness which requires a mediator (see Chapter 7; then see 1 Timothy 2:5 and Hebrews 12:24).

- Bokos sprinkle blood on their doorposts to protect the home from evil, then read Exodus 12:13 NKJV: "Now the blood shall be a sign for you on the houses where you are. And when I see the blood, I will pass over you; and the plague shall not be on you to destroy you when I strike the land of Egypt."

- The Quechua Festival of *Tapacari*, in the Department of Cochabamba, Bolivia, where a person will wear a thick red woolen cape upon which other people will beat with a stick. The red representing blood shed, the ingredient needed to bring back harmony, peace and order to their world. Compare Colossians 1:20 NKJV, "…and by him to reconcile all things to Himself, by Him, whether things on earth or things in heaven, having made peace through the blood of His cross." Other symbolic scriptural analogies involving blood sacrifice could be derived from this custom.

- Sorcerer's power to bring sickness and death by a variety of means, i.e., heating an iron in the fire, winding a string around a goat's bone, the locking of a padlock, etc. Speak then of the power of Jesus' word to heal the sick and raise the dead, His use of mud to heal the blind and by His word He cast out demons, etc.

- Inquire as to the cycles of life rituals they perform to appease the evil spirits. Then, announce the ultimate ritual of Jesus' death provided by God to propitiate for man's sin of worshiping the creation and refusing to even acknowledge the Creator.

- Talk to them about the animist's desire to have a harmonious relationship with powerful evil forces. Then inform them that the almighty Creator God desires a relationship with men which will endue them with power greater than Satan's.

- Many animistic societies fear the location of crossroads or places where paths cross. They will place a variety of sacrifices (i.e., grain, kola nuts, coins, cotton, chickens, etc.) at those places to placate the resident spirits. A discussion about this topic could easily lead into a presentation about the cross (the intersection of two pieces of wood) of Christ, its 'crossroads' location outside the city and the necessity of that sacrifice.

- Animists rituals are to appease the spirits. Jesus' sacrifice was a ritual to propitiate the offended Creator God.

- In Don Richardson's book, *The Peace Child*, other redemptive analogies can be found that may be similar to the customs of the people among whom the missionary may be living.

With an understanding of the beliefs and customs of the receptors, the gospel messenger can 'break the animist's code,' then encode the gospel message in terms of their world view and gain immediate access to their thinking by the use of these communication bridges. Paul's bridge to the Athenians was the "Unknown God." Find those cultural equivalents in your area of ministry and you may be encouraged as Paul was when they said, "We want to hear you again on this subject" (Acts 17:32).

STUDY THE WORD

Since the encounter with animists is really about spiritual warfare, it is imperative for the gospel communicator to prepare by saturating himself in the Word concerning the schemes of the devil, but more importantly, God's plan and provision of power to defeat the evil one. Here a word study of such words like power, authority, dominion, exorcise, Satan, devil, demon, sorcerers, power of and fear of death, darkness, deliver, the state of the lost, defeat and victory, etc., would be most profitable.

The reader would do well to study the Old Testament encounters of God's people with evil spiritual forces (i.e., Elijah and the prophets of Baal, Saul and the witch of Endor, etc.) and God's commands against all forms of sorcery.

Follow this up with a study of Jesus' ministry of power over disease, death, demons, nature and mankind's sinful nature.

Examine how Jesus after His resurrection and ascension, endued His followers with His power and authority (Matt. 28:18-20) and the Holy Spirit's power (Acts 1:8) to perpetuate the preaching of the gospel of the kingdom of God until the end of the age. One cannot read the accounts of Jesus' activities in the Gospels and of those of his disciples in the Book of Acts without being in awe of the uninhibited demonstration of God's supernatural power. Most Westerners easily consent to the truth of this power intellectually because it is in God's Holy Spirit-inspired record. By the same token, some evangelicals dismiss the reality of miracles or of the supernatural happening today. Having come from a scientific, secular world view myself, which separates the natural and supernatural, I struggle at times to reconcile that Western thinking with my personal experience with the reality of supernatural events, both good and evil, in Africa. This question then arises in my mind: if we doubt the reality of the supernatural happening today, can we still be effective gospel messengers of deliverance to people who live their daily lives under the dominion of supernatural evil spiritual powers?

(For a list of scriptures dealing with this subject, see Appendix B.)

PRESENTATION

THE GOSPEL FROM GENESIS

For the initial presentation of the gospel to animists, I would suggest the missionary begin as I did in the "Story of Baba," which illustrates man's dilemma of being in a daily struggle with evil spiritual powers and needing empowerment to be able to cope with life. By illustrating this dependence on the spirits "without criticizing the horrors and moral carelessness of heathen life," Warneck suggests, "the missionary will implant an aversion to them by these stories"[4] of Jesus' power from the Gospels. The use of communication bridges (i.e., some of the sacrifices to appease the evil spirits or to protect them from their enemy's curses, etc.) will have a complementary effect rather than a message of condemnation on animist's beliefs and practices.

Then I would describe how man was originally created with power as previously described in chapter one. This naturally leads to the story of how man lost his power through the one act of taking the forbidden fruit; an action demonstrating the rejection of God's authority and a commitment to Satan's.

Profiting from their belief that offending the spirits will bring retribution, tell the story of God's curses on His creation. At this point inquire about some of their practices relating to the spirits (i.e., for a pregnancy, good crops, funerals, etc.) to get them thinking about their subjection to spirits, and their experience with the evil spirit's ability to give or withhold *Alafia* from them. Warneke reminds us that a "decisive influence in bringing the heathen to Christianity is their experience of the impotence of the heathen sanctuaries and idols."[5] The testimony of Baa Abram, an elder in the Segbana church, supports that statement. Throughout his lifetime he had been blessed with fifteen children. In spite of numerous consultations with diviners and endless sacrifices made to multitudinous spirits, and to his heart breaking with dismay, only one of these survived to adulthood.

The next step is to inform them that the very objects and spirits that they worship are the very ones that God cursed. As if that were not bad enough, they have neglected even to acknowledge who the Creator is and what He has done. Could it be that they have offended Him by never making a sacrifice to Him? Perhaps like Baba, they will ask you, "How do we make a sacrifice to God?"

But before pursuing the answer, lead up to it by telling them stories of the power of Jesus over sickness, death, nature and demons. "The glad message of God's revealed deeds," Warneck hints, "carries in itself the power of overcoming heathenism."[6] "We only bear witness to its truth," says Dr. Nida, "for it is the Spirit of God that directly communicates and mediates this divine word."[7] Once convinced by the Holy Spirit of Christ's power, the animist will open himself to allow this power to pervade his whole life.

POWER ENCOUNTER

Animism is a power religion whose source of power is not human, but rather supernatural and evil (Eph. 6:12). Christianity is a power religion whose source of power is the almighty Creator God who holds the ultimate power even over death.

When a messenger of the gospel confronts the animistic system, little short of a demonstration of the greater power of Jesus will convince the animist that he will be "...kept by the power of God..." (1 Pet. 1:5 NKJV) from the vengeance of the spirit forces. Dr. Tippett rightly explains that "The conversion of animists is not a passage from non-faith to faith. It is a passage from wrong faith to right faith, from the false god to the true God."[8] "It has to be an act of faith..." when animists "...are confident that the power of their new Lord is greater"[9] and "...they no longer fear the old gods."[10]

Elijah's power encounter with the prophets of Baal on Mt. Carmel (1 Kings. 18:16-39) and the Apostles' encounters with evil in the book of Acts certainly evidenced the power of God working through His servants. We Western missionaries sometimes have lively debates concerning the validity and availability of that power to us today. I agree with Dr. Steyne that "...little headway will be made in establishing vital and truly biblical Christianity among animistic peoples" ...unless... "...Christian workers seek those opportunities where they can give a clear demonstration that Jesus Christ is indeed Lord of all and over all other powers."[11]

Without any statistical back up, my impression is that the vast majority of first generation Boko believers "...turned to God from idols to serve the living and true God..." (1 Thes. 1:9), as the result of a power encounter. Up to this time, I had no prior understanding of power encounters. However, after hearing the conversion experiences of Boko believers, I became very aware that the power encounter was their way of discerning truth.

Here is the account of a happening in the village of Salonzi where prior to the presentation of the gospel most of the young to middle aged men had already made a group decision to convert to Islam. Then along came a group of young Boko Christians singing and announcing the good news of Jesus Christ. One of their talks had to do with John 14:6b, where Jesus says "...no one comes to the Father except through me." The Holy Spirit burdened these villagers with the thought that there is only one way to get to God or heaven, the Jesus Way. These men believed they had already taken God's Way in Islam, but they were perplexed that there might possibly be another way. Reasoning that there could only be one true way they decided to settle the matter on a hunt.

They designated the kill of a roan antelope to be indicative that Islam was the true way. If they got a hartebeest then they would know that the Jesus Way was the one true way. Let me insert here that the roan are the more numerous, more curious and therefore easier to hunt. The hartebeests being fewer and more easily frightened off are much more difficult to hunt. By the end of the day on this hunt they had killed two hartebeests, no roan. The dilemma was indisputably resolved; they all rejected Islam and took the Jesus Way. This spiritual power encounter revealed to them the belief system which was more powerful, therefore the true way. From now on they were 'Jesus

People.' Regular services were begun and literacy classes started along with the teaching of songs and the scriptural principles of the Jesus Way. As they grew in the knowledge of their relationship with the Lord, this group of believers became one of the more dynamic Boko churches.

Interestingly, Sara, the first baptized woman Boko believer, came to the Lord after telling Jesus to verify that He was all powerful and therefore the true way to God by seeing to it that she became pregnant with her new husband and that the baby be a girl. The believers in her village prayed with her that she would become pregnant. Nine months later, she gave birth to twin girls. God was faithful and able to meet the present needs of these people. He brought them into a relationship with Himself through Jesus according to the Boko understanding of the spiritual world. Sara became a godly woman, strong in her faith and trust in the Lord to provide for her, protect her from her former evil spiritual world and her nephew who sought to kill her with fire and curses. One of her twins eventually married a Boko evangelist, to serve the Lord in an unreached village. The other married and became the leader of the women in her local church.

Neither the Salonzi hunt nor Sara's pregnancy was the typical Western evangelistic method of inviting people to come to Christ. Nevertheless, this was the way God reached into these animists' blinded hearts to bring them from darkness to the kingdom of Light.

Dr. Tippett succinctly describes what I believe takes place in the context of an animist's commitment to 'take the Jesus Way.'

There is to be "...a change of loyalty..." involving "an act of commitment and an act of rejection" in making this decision. The symbolic rejection of the old way not only involves a religious encounter, but thereafter serves as a continual reminder of the act of rejection that alone can save the convert from syncretism or polytheism. The biblical evidence of this demand for commitment to Christ in some form of dramatic encounter shows the converts that the old way no longer has power over them.[12]
The power encounter is the key step that leads to conversion.

After having talked with Westerners about the power encounter experience, this question has been raised, "What if the power encounter does not work?" This response is pretty typically Western, reflecting the scientific-secular world view. However, because fatalism plays a significant part in the animist's world view, their response probably would be, "It just wasn't meant to be."

The purpose of these power encounters was not manipulative, but rather to determine truth. The power/authority element of the animist's world view engendered the need for the power encounter. Their world view has enculturated them to react this way. Hence, the question, "What if it does not work?" is a non-question in the animist's culture. The encounter will always work for them one way or another and their fatalism will approve the answer. As the animist convert grows in the knowledge of his relationship with the powerful and loving God who has a plan for his life, many aspects of his old life will fade away.

The Westerner's responsibility is to patiently endeavor to

understand their thinking and encourage them as the Holy Spirit teaches them the new way.

Now let's talk next about the conversion experience of animists.

CONVERSION

God's grace and confirmation from the scriptures enabled me to conquer the fear I had that no Bokos, because of some of their heathen practices, would ever become Christians. That issue having been settled, I then wondered what would indicate to me when a Boko had truly taken the Jesus Way. After struggling with that question for a period of time, the Holy Spirit directed me to the answer in the Word in 1 Thessalonians 1:7-9, where Paul informs the Thessalonian believers about the impact of their witness to their faith:

> And so you became a model to all believers in Macedonia and Achaia. The Lord's message rang out from you...your faith in God has become known everywhere. They tell how you turned to God from idols to serve the living and true God, and to wait for His Son from heaven.

The key phrases here are, "...your faith in God..." and "...turned to God from idols." My 'paraphrased, amplified version' of these verses put into the animistic context would read something like this:

> You animistic Thessalonians turned from, repented of your submission to and your worship of spirit beings and having faith in the true God's power to

91

deliver you from the power of these spirits, submitted
yourselves to the authority of the living Creator God
and then out of gratitude for His deliverance offered
to serve Him, while waiting for the appearance of
His Son from heaven.

I needed some indication of the Bokos' conversion experience
so that I would know when to begin to teach them about the
biblical concepts of sin, salvation, Jesus, the Savior and other
truths. So when someone offered personal information
corresponding to the key phrase, "...turned to God from
idols...", I considered that individual to have been converted.
For example, when one of the followers gave testimony that
they had refused the family's entreaty to go to the diviner and
make the prescribed sacrifice for their sick son's healing, but
instead, they were trusting in Jesus' power to heal him, this
was a demonstration of the rejection of the old way and a
commitment to the new way.

Warneck defines conversion in the animist's context as,
The knowledge of God which comes to them from
His revealed acts delivers them from bondage. The
insurmountable wall that rises up between the
heathen and God is not sin, as among ourselves
(not in the first place at any rate); it is the kingdom
of darkness in which they are bound. The animist
enters into a faith relationship with the almighty
Creator God by hearing of His powerful acts and
this sets him free from the power and fear that has
bound him. The way back to God has been found.

> They decide at this point to follow Jesus not as the
> Savior from sin, but as their deliverer from the
> kingdom of darkness.[13]

This idea is reinforced by the fact that the original sin was not about the usual list of sins (i.e., lying, stealing, adultery, etc.), but rather about who was going to be the lord of Adam and Eve's lives. To whose authority and control would they submit? Their disobedience was an act of rejection of God's lordship and a commitment to Satan's authority. This led to the worship of created things and subjection to Satan's "...spiritual forces of evil..." (Eph. 6:12), rather than to the Creator. Thus came about the development of the world view, the beliefs and practices of the power religion we know as animism. So, just as Adam and Eve became alienated from God by rejecting His authority and accepting Satan's authority, accordingly, when animists reject Satan's authority and accept God's authority, they have come back 'full circle' into the originally designed trusting relationship with God. Warneck explains it like this,

> But the fact that they no longer have any desire to
> serve idols or Satan, but the living God who offers
> them grace and forgiveness of sin in Christ, shows
> that they have experienced a true conversion and
> that of a primary kind.[14]

In the animist's world view, the power encounter functions as the step of affirmation distinguishing the truth from the lie, the true way versus the false, and the greater power from the lesser. The truth of this experience now empowers the animist to exchange the lie of Satan for the truth of God and worship and serve the Creator rather than the creature. The animists' conversion experience at this level of their knowledge of the gospel involves a repentance from the sin of not acknowledging God, though they knew Him, nor glorifying Him as God, nor being thankful, and of worshiping the creature instead of the Creator (see Rom. 1:21, 25 NKJV). Hesselgrave supports this view in his biblical definition of conversion also appropriate for the animist:

> Conversion is an act of the believer which follows repentance in which he turns to God in such a fashion that the beliefs and the practices of the old religion are completely forsaken and the grace of God becomes observable in his life.[15]

The act of repentance, according to Warneck resulted in God's two-fold gift to animists: "...communion with the living God and deliverance from idolatry."[16] Thanks to the powerful gospel of Jesus Christ, God has been reinstated as the animists' Lord. They decide to follow Jesus at this point not as the Savior from sin, but as their deliverer from the kingdom of darkness.[17]

"But wait a minute," you say, "you haven't even mentioned the sacrificial death of Jesus on the cross, the shedding of His blood for the remission of our sins, or Jesus' death, burial and resurrection. How can you unilaterally declare them converted? Nobody can be saved without knowing this!"

If this is what you are thinking, your questions are legitimate. You should be asking them. So let's go on.

JESUS THE SAVIOR

Lest the reader has slipped back into the Western theological approach of the 'salvation from sin alone' theme mentioned earlier, I would remind you that my purpose throughout the book has been to present the gospel in the terms of the animist's setting; to accommodate his understanding, yet still be biblically sound and relevant. That is why the subject of the Saviorhood of Jesus has not come up until now.

Warneck explains the process of the animist's salvation from sin this way:

> Now God has conquered the powers of darkness in a heathen heart and brought that heart into connection with Himself; but sin has not yet left the field...the consciousness of sin is only gradually awakened.[17]

Another way of saying it could be: "The heathen heart, as we have seen it, is reached not from the moral side, but rather from the religious side. The heathen has gained a living relation to God and a conviction through Christ of his own sinfulness."[19] Warneck continues: "Moral growth is slow," nevertheless, "the grosser heathen abominations [practices] certainly are given up at once, as soon as the heathen know the true God...."[20] To put it in another way, "The deliverance from Satanic powers, and their renunciation of the kingdom of darkness is effected at once; however, the knowledge of their own unworthiness is gradual."[21] It seems then that the animist's God consciousness, lost by the "...wickedness of men who suppress the truth by their wickedness" (Rom. 1:18), becomes liberated by their relationship with the Creator.

95

Somewhere in the gospel presentation process of moving from their dilemma (the order can change according to individual circumstances), to the communication bridges, to the gospel from Genesis, to the power of Jesus, to the power encounter, to conversion, the animist becomes aware that he has offended the Creator by sacrificing to His creation, but never to the Creator Himself. Since animists' definition of sin, in part, is a transgression against the requirements of the spiritual world, the transgression against the Creator is then understood by animists as sin. It is on that basis that they can accept the fact that they are sinners. This disclosure evoked that spontaneous response from Baba at Belabelana, "No wonder we don't have *Alafia*!" followed by the question, "How, then, do I make a sacrifice to God?" His religion had taught him that an offended spirit (in this case God) must always be appeased with the proper ritual precisely performed. For it is the only way *Alafia* (order, balance and harmony) can be restored.

Now is the time to introduce the biblical concept of the Creator, not only being powerful, but also holy and loving.

Because His holiness has been defiled by man's sin, God has decreed that only the ritual of a perfect blood sacrifice will propitiate His wrath (Rom. 3:24,25; 5:9). Since "It is not possible that the blood of bulls and goats could take away sins" (Heb 10:4 NKJV), and because of His love (Eph. 2:4) for powerless mankind, God provided the only acceptable and sinless ritual, the sacrifice for man's transgressions "... through the sacrifice of the body of Jesus Christ once for all" (Heb. 10:10). Paul corroborates this truth in Romans 5:8,9,11:

> But God demonstrates His own love for us in this:
> While we were still sinners, Christ died for us. Since
> we have been justified by his blood, how much
> more shall we be saved from God's wrath through
> him! Not only is this so, but we also rejoice in God
> through our Lord Jesus Christ, through whom we
> have now received the reconciliation.

The way the Bokos determine if a sacrificial chicken will be acceptable to the spirits is to put its head under water. If the chicken withdraws its head from the water and shakes it's head, the witch doctor knows that the spirits will accept it. If not, another chicken must be obtained. Similarly, but in a more powerful way, God confirmed His acceptance of Jesus' sacrifice for mankind's transgressions by raising Jesus from the dead. By the transaction of Jesus' death and resurrection, a number of things were brought to pass that would reverse the effects of God's curses, some immediately and others in the future:

- **Death:** defeated and life restored (Rom.5:17; Eph. 2:1; 1 Cor. 15:22; Heb. 2:14,15).
- **Creation:** all creation is to be reconciled to God (Rom. 8:19-21; Col. 1:20; Eph. 1:10).
- **Alienation:** man is restored to fellowship with God (Rom. 5:10, 2 Cor. 5:18,19, Eph. 2:13, Col. 1:21,22).
- **Judgment for Disobedience:** forgiveness of sin (Acts 26:18; Col. 1:14; 2:13).
- **Separation From God:** from the kingdom of darkness into the kingdom of the Son of his love (Col. 1:13,21).
- **Foreigners:** citizens in God's community (Acts 26:18; Eph. 2:12,19; Col.1:13; 1 Pet. 2:9).

- **Rejection:** peace (Alafia) with God (Rom. 5:1; 1:20).
- **Judgment:** from condemnation to justification (Rom. 5:16,18; 8:1).
- **Degradation:** hope of complete redemption for believers and all creation (Rom. 8:18-23).
- **Evil Powers:** all of Satan's authority and power will come to an end (1 Cor. 15:24-28).

If animists will first make that faith decision to turn to God from idols, from the power of Satan to God, then their futile thinking and darkened hearts (Rom. 1:21) likewise, will be turned from darkness to light as the Holy Spirit opens their spiritual eyes (Acts 26:18; 1 Pet. 2:9). At that time, they are freed to understand the reality of a relationship with the loving, powerful Creator God. And Jesus, their deliverer from Satan also becomes their Savior from sin, the embodiment of love to the love-starved animists' hearts.

"Those who advance to a knowledge of sin," asserts Warneck, "are the true Christians."[22] They recognize their deliverance from the spiritual powers, plus they understand that it is their sin that stands between them and their relationship with God. The knowledge of God's love in Christ compels them to begin a new life and seek cleansing for their sin. They are then both born-again and delivered.

PRACTICAL RESULTS

MORALITY

Interestingly, I observed many of the born-again and delivered Boko Christians who formerly had no concept of the biblical concept of sin, nor the knowledge of the possibility of a relationship with the Creator, began to develop a moral conscience. They realized that just as offending the spirits would cause disorder in their former religion, now as a believer in the Jesus Way, sin would endanger their relationship with God. This compelled them to turn to Jesus and His Word for power to overcome sin and maintain their relationship with God. Davidi, one of the first group of Bokos to be baptized, would declare over and over whenever a conflict arose between his culture and the teaching of God's Word, "Whatever Jesus' Word says, we'll do it." His was a commitment to trust in the power of Jesus to enable him to obey Him in all things.

COURAGE

Persecution was a given for these Boko believers. When they rejected the authority of the spirits and turned to God, this decision, according to animists' perception of their religion, affected the believer's whole family and sometimes the whole village and possibly the whole tribe. Understandably, each tribe and even each region within a tribe has its own spiritual powers and beings.

To illustrate how this works, I like to think of the animistic religion as a globe, a closed system with all the people living inside it. The system is self-contained and maintains its harmony and order, *Alafia*, only by strict compliance of each member of the society to the rules of the spiritual forces. Theoretically, this alone will keep the spirits happy. When any member or members of the society reject the authority of the spirits, or offend them, this 'opens a window' in the globe, creating weakness, imbalance and disunity in the spiritual system. The spirits rally to create chaos and fear in their subjects in order to enforce the order and submission they require.

Of course, it is the Christians that 'open the window' by their nonadherence to the rules of the capricious spirits. Though Christians are protected from the retribution of the evil spirits, they are nevertheless, the ones who are responsible for arousing the anger of the spirits who then inflict the non-believing family members with calamity, such as sickness, death or bad crops. At this point, the family unleashes its fear of the spirits by persecuting the Christian members with threats, insults, black magic and curses or as in Davidi's case, by physically taking away his wife and children.

I never ceased to be amazed at Davidi's capacity to suffer for Christ. He patiently accepted the persecution and reproach out of gratitude for all that Jesus did for him. He not only endured it, but his faith grew as he composed the words and music of many of the original Boko hymns. There was a time when I apologized to him for causing his pain, since I was the one who introduced him to the Jesus Way. He quickly responded with, "Don't feel badly for me. They can take everybody and everything I have away from me, but they will never be able to take the *Alafia*, the peace, that is in my heart." He was poor in this world's goods, but rich in a childlike faith in his Creator.

LITERACY

One of the first jobs I had upon arrival in Segbana was to produce an alphabet for the unwritten Boko language using the characters from the International Phonetic Alphabet. The ultimate goal was to translate the Bible into their language. The intermediate step was to produce primers to teach them to read their own language and then to teach them to teach others. This program was modeled after the *How To Teach One and Win One For Christ* literacy system originated by Dr. Frank C. Laubach, known as the 'Apostle of Literacy.'

When a literacy program was offered to them, they were quick to respond. Their conversion from darkness to light (2 Cor. 4:6), the moving power of the love of God in their hearts, a cultural belief in the power of words, and a hunger to read 'God's Word,' awakened within them the desire to take advantage of this opportunity to become literate. In fact, in one village, it was the local witch doctor who not only enthusiastically pressed the village people, young and old, men and women, to attend reading classes, but also to construct a building of their own to serve as a classroom and for a place of worship. Seriously, my theology would not have allowed me to choose the witch doctor, the spiritual emissary of my spiritual enemy, Satan, to be the facilitator of the gospel ministry among the Bokos. This became one of many incidents in my experience where God took the progress of this ministry out of my hands and interjected His way of building His Church.

Though it was beyond my comprehension, I finally determined that my responsibility was to be faithful, trust Him and follow His sovereign initiatives. I also learned that I did not have to be "…ashamed of the gospel because it is the power of God for the salvation of everyone who believes" (Rom. 1:16).

In summary, we have considered how the lies of Satan, the god of this evil world, have kept mankind in bondage to himself through fear. He has blinded the minds of those who don't believe, lest the light of the powerful, liberating truth of the gospel pierce the darkness of the human heart. We have been made aware of man's vain efforts to control his own destiny by seeking empowerment from the emissaries of the evil one, only to fall prey to his sly schemes. But then, the almighty Creator God who in the beginning said, "Let there be light," caused the Good News to shine into men's hearts to let them see Jesus, whose name, power and authority is supreme over all creation. By reason of his faith in the powerful gospel of Jesus Christ, mankind's frustrated search for empowerment from created spiritual beings ceases. Mankind's need and desire for *Alafia* finally finds fulfillment in his relationship with the ultimate and eternal source of empowerment, Jesus. When man becomes reconciled to His Creator, he is at peace. His quest for power has been satisfied.

As the resurrection power of Christ continued to deliver men and women, boys and girls from Satan's bondage, it became evident that godly leaders would need to be prepared to provide teaching, guidance, encouragement and direction to the community of Christians that the Lord was establishing. How that happened will be found in Part II that follows.

Chapter 4—Notes:

1. Warneck, John, *The Living Christ and Dying Heathenism* (Grand Rapids, MI: Baker Book House, 1954) p.117.

2. Tippett, Alan, *Introduction to Missiology* (Pasadena, CA: William Carey Library, 1987) p. 328.

3. Warneck, 1954, p. 253.

4. Ibid., p. 278.

5. Ibid., p. 216.

6. Ibid., p. 232.

7. Nida, Eugene A., *Mission and Message: The Communication of the Christian Faith* (New York: Harper and Row Publishers, 1960) p. 229.

8. Tippett, 1987, p. 83.

9. Ibid., p. 84

10. Ibid., p. 83.

11. Steyne, Philip M., *Gods Of Power* (Columbia, SC: Impact International Foundation) p. 19.

12. Tippett, 1987, pp. 328, 329.

13. Warneck, 1954, pp. 232, 233.

14. Ibid., pp. 246, 247.

15. Hesselgrave, David J., *Planting Churches Cross-Culturally: A Guide for Home and Foreign Missions* (Grand Rapids, MI. 49506: Baker Book House, 1980) p. 235.

16. Warneck, 1954, p. 251.

17. To reinforce the conversion decision of turning to God from idols, each baptismal candidate renounced all previous association with or participation in spirit worship, claimed the blood of Jesus for forgiveness and protection, then vowed from then on to have nothing to do with that system of beliefs and its practices. They confessed Jesus Lord and the Creator their God.

18. Warneck, 1954, p. 247.

19. Ibid., p. 267.

20. Ibid., p. 268.

21. Ibid., p. 265.

22. Ibid., p. 264.

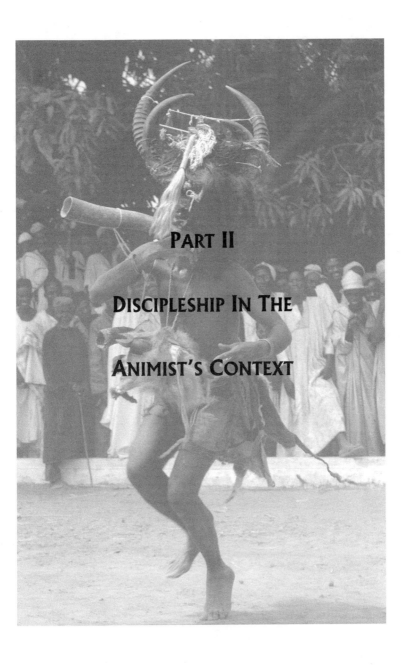

PART II

DISCIPLESHIP IN THE

ANIMIST'S CONTEXT

INTRODUCTION

The first attempt to provide any kind of discipleship training among the Boko Christians began with 'Short Term Bible Schools' in the mid to late 1960's.

During the dry season when the farm work had slowed down, all believers, literate or not, were invited to come to study the Word in the village where we resided. The first year was a one week course studying the Gospel of Mark. The Epistle of Titus was studied the following year. Up to that time, these two New Testament books were the only ones translated.

While we were on furlough, our new missionary colleague[1] followed up on this by establishing a 'Preacher's Training School,' which initially met two days a week, every other week. With so little scriptural input, we realized that ultimately the Holy Spirit and the reality of Christ's power in their daily lives would have to be instrumental in keeping the early believers true to their commitment to God.

Concurrent with these Bible teaching opportunities, a believer's literacy program was initiated. We limited the teaching to adults at first.[2] Then we taught them how to teach others.

Motivated by the Holy Spirit, scores seized the opportunity to be 'schooled' and especially to learn to read and study God's Word in their own language.

The believer's keen desire to learn to read and to know God's Word made us think seriously about the need to provide advanced training in the Word just for the village church leaders.

It was at this critical juncture in the development of Boko church leadership that God providentially brought us in contact with Don Jacobs, a missionary with the Eastern Mennonite Mission, who recounted a very significant incident from his experience teaching theology in a seminary in Tanzania, East Africa.

Don recounted how he had felt pretty good about the previous semester's accomplishments. He had completed all of the academic material prescribed in the course syllabus. The theology came right out of classical Western theology textbooks, which start with the doctrine of God and end up with eschatology. The African students seemed mature in their approach to the work. They wrote commendable papers on a variety of subjects. The feedback in their exams was correct; right out of the textbooks. That is, they had absorbed the course work and given it back, properly, just as it had been given to them. Don was pleased that his students had responded so well. He felt that his mission had been successfully accomplished. Then he asked the class if they had any questions. At this point, a graduating senior laid bare a very personal, practical, yet theological problem. He explained it this way:

I am the oldest son of my aging father. I am the

only Christian in my family. After my graduation, I will be going home to live in my father's house. When my father dies, I, the oldest son, will fall heir to his material things, but more importantly, I will become responsible for the welfare of my family, all of whom are pagan. One of these responsibilities will be to see that at his death, my father's spirit is sent off to the place of our family ancestors. This can be done only by following the prescribed pagan rites and ceremonies.

As a Christian, how should I deal with these pagan ritual requirements? Should I refuse to have a part in these rites? Should I absent myself from the village at this time? Should I provide the sacrificial cow whose blood will be shed to assure my father's spirit's passage to the land of his ancestors, but I, myself not take part in the ceremony? Should I be there just to provide food and housing for the many family members and guests who will assemble at our house for the 3 to 4 days of funeral ceremonies? How can I show respect for father and family and yet be uncompromisingly faithful to my Lord and Savior?

Don was shocked to realize that the time tested, well organized, balanced, Western theology had not spoken to some of the basic issues of the people whose world view is animistic. Because of this, Don felt like the time put into this course had been wasted; he had failed his students.

Evaluating the course in retrospect, Don concluded that his teaching of theology had been Western as to:

Approach: that theology begins with the doctrine of God and the rational proofs for His existence, whereas animists already believe in a Creator God, the spirit world, and do not have to be convinced of the existence of the supernatural.

Content: the study of predestination, for example, included supra and infralapsarianism: a dispute which happened during early Reformation days in Geneva that was not relevant to converted animists.

Pedagogy: This method of study not only categorizes, but also teaches theology in blocks of seemingly unrelated and independent information in specified periods of time. Whereas, the animists world view perceives existence, both animate and inanimate objects holistically and interrelated. As to pedagogical method, the non-Western way is to teach information as related events occur.

In each instance above, he concluded that there was no cultural or linguistic bridge to provide a way for animists to understand Western theology in terms of their own view of existence. Nor does their tribal history nor their world view provide a clue to help them understand Western-oriented theology. In other words, the Western theological approach was giving answers to questions they were not asking.

If given the opportunity to do it over again in Africa, Don indicated that as to content, he would not start the study of theology with the Western view of the doctrine of God. Rather, he would start with the familiar: the animistic man's dilemma. That he is in a struggle with evil spiritual powers from whom he must seek personal spiritual empowerment *to* successfully attain the state of *'Alafia'* in this life.

The time had arrived in the brief history of the Boko church to provide a discipleship training program for first generation church leaders. In order to take full advantage of this unique opportunity to establish a biblically and culturally relevant model, I took seriously Don's advice to contextualize the study program.

What did that mean biblically? Just as we had observed how Paul presented the gospel in a variety of cultural contexts, I went to the scriptures to discover Paul's methodology for discipling first generation believers.

First, I discovered some of the things he did not do: he did not establish a resident Bible School, nor did he develop a standardized curriculum universally appropriate to all believers everywhere.

But what did he do? He was a 'circuit rider,' moving from group to group of believers, discipling them at their location, then moving on. This activity recorded in the Acts of The Apostles is described as Paul's three missionary journeys. As to curriculum or content, Paul taught each group according to their level of Christian maturity (1 Cor. 3:1-3) and the issues they were dealing with at the time (Gal. 1:6). Then out of love and concern for their spiritual well being, he revisited some churches and/or wrote letters (the Epistles) to follow up on his previous teaching. He was not content just to send a generic letter to all the churches covering all their current problems. Rather, he addressed the current and specific problems of each particular group. Thus, we have the Epistles to individual churches, each addressing a particular theme, e.g. legalism to the Galatians, immorality to the Corinthians, etc.[4]

In summary, Paul's method includes: 1) teach them where they are; 2) teach each group according to their local problems and level of spiritual maturity; 3) plan follow-up visits.

Giving serious consideration to Paul's model and Don Jacob's experience, I began to pray and ponder the implications of adapting these concepts to disciple first generation church leaders in terms of their context. That would include: 1) their location; 2) the biblical teachings both related to and new to their world view; 3) their traditional teaching method; 4) their pedagogical expectancy and 5) their social situation.

Yet, there was more to take into account: the reality that these believers were just literate[3] in their own language and that the translation of the New Testament was still in process. It was important to remember that most of these men were married with children and still a vital part of a subsistence family farming community. All of them were already serving in positions of leadership in their village church.

We concluded that Paul's model was relevant to the Boko setting. We just had to be flexible and trust the Lord to help us work out the details.

The purpose of this section of the book is to share with the reader the practical ways the Lord provided cultural and biblical direction to meet this challenge of discipling Boko Christian leadership in their cultural context.

INTRODUCTION—NOTES:

1. Ross Jones, my colleague, not only established this Preacher's Training School, but along with his faithful translation team translated the entire Bible into the Boko language.

2. Adults were taught to read first because: 1) traditionally the adults are the teachers; 2) since children learn more quickly, adults could be embarrassed, intimidated, discouraged and drop out; 3) adult teachers assure the future of a literacy program.

3. See Appendix C.

4. 'Just literate' means that the reader has completed the two basic primers, a couple of graded readers and learned to write.

CHAPTER 5

TRADITIONAL AFRICAN EDUCATION

An unprecedented opportunity was before me to establish a discipleship methodology based on biblical principles, as modeled by Paul and that was at the same time relevant to the local Boko setting.

The traditional Boko educational system (as in most of Africa and other parts of the developing world) was oral, not having a written language. The teaching time frame was continuous, based not on a block of classroom time like a semester, but rather a flow of teaching with topics determined by the season of the year and what was happening in their lives. This included climatic seasons, annual rites and holidays, market days and emergency events (i.e., birth, sickness, death). Daily life was the classroom. The information shared and activities a person participated in were according to the age and the ability of the individual.

Reverend Victor Musa, a Nigerian church leader, informed me that daily events as they occurred became the 'curriculum' of teachable moments. That included on-site, hands-on instruction such as: how to hoe corn rows, how to make a sacrifice to idols or how to identify both human and animal footprints. Then, there were the unplanned events to be explained, such as death or the sudden arrival of a chief.

The teachers were the adults, male and female, usually from, but not limited to, one's extended family. In addition to the hands-on method of instruction by demonstration, the adults were role models of their activities, which were then imitated by the students. Indirect learning came as children sat around the fireside listening (sometimes eavesdropping) to adult discussions, the singing of songs, the reciting of riddles and proverbs.

The traditional African educational system can be described as family centered, with adults, formally and informally teaching a flow of information appropriate to the student's age concerning all daily aspects of daily life as events occur.

Their communication style is high-context (HC). Edward T. Hall, renowned for his ideas on cross-cultural communication, says,

> A high-context (HC) communication or message is one in which most of the information is either in the physical context or internalized in the person, while very little is in the coded, explicit, transmitted part of the message. A low-context (LC) communication is just the opposite; i.e., the mass of information is vested in the explicit code.[1]

LC communication expresses a message to the finest detail, the 'jot and tittle,' so to speak. However, in HC communication, meaning is deduced from the context of the situation with minimal information passed on. An individual in a group setting then draws his conclusions/makes decisions in his own mind based on the consensus of opinions expressed by the group. Little detail is provided. For example, at a church elder's meeting which I attended, two subjects were being discussed with decisions to be made on both. One was organizing the congregation to work in the church peanut field. The other was to clean up the church property. As the discussion developed, I noticed that after having discussed briefly the peanut field problem, they switched to the church cleanup issue without having arrived at any conclusion on either problem. The discussion continued in this manner for a time, when all of a sudden, they all got up and headed for the door. I panicked. I was frustrated.

I blurted out, "Wait a minute. You haven't decided anything, yet!" To which they responded, "What's the matter, Pasitee (my name), don't you understand our language?"

Obviously, the problem was mine! Language was not the problem, but rather their decision making style was different. I was trying to process the event through my LC Western grid; the details of *Robert's Rules of Order* (a motion, a discussion and a vote, etc.). Fortunately, there was a 'Barnabas' who lovingly came alongside and explained the details to me. This event was 'stored' for future reference. Nevertheless, in retrospect, I have to wonder just how much my frustration level could have been reduced had I known about HC and LC communication styles.

Another aspect of the African learning style is that they learn better in groups, rather than one-on-one. African society is group-oriented and interdependent. There are few secrets in this society. Little is private. So, when it comes to discussing what to Westerners would be considered very private, the discussion of intimate things in their peer group is minimal.

Let me summarize the factors that are transferable between Paul's methods and the traditional Boko educational system:

	Paul's	Boko
Location:	taught in their villages	taught at home
Curriculum:	specific current issues	specific current events
	according to maturity of student	according to maturity of student
Time frame:	determined by teacher/student	intermittent, continuous availability to adulthood
	follow up by letters or visits over a long period of time	repetition of information
Teachers:	mature believers	adults
Methods:	role model to emulate	role model to emulate
	mentor young believers	work with and teach alongside
	direct teaching of the Word	young included in adult discussions
Numbers:	groups and individuals	groups, rarely individuals

These comparisons gave us assurance that Paul's methods would be practical and beneficial in discipling first generation believers and more importantly, church leadership in terms relevant to their culture.

Having chosen to emulate the African educational system, which is initiated as events, problems, circumstances and traditions happen and immediately implemented, this discipling process for the believers and church leaders was labeled, **Event-Oriented Discipling**.

CHAPTER 5—NOTES:

1. Hall, Edward T., *Beyond Culture* (New York: Anchor Books, Doubleday, 1989) p. 91.

CHAPTER 6

EVENT-ORIENTED DISCIPLING

WHY?

"Why go with such a slow system of learning, this Event-Oriented Discipling," the Western reader might ask, "when a resident Bible School setting would transmit biblical knowledge more rapidly and get the evangelists out into the field that much sooner?"

This is a legitimate question from an 'outsider' who is driven by the urgency to store up blocks of biblical information whether currently applicable or not. However, for one who sees the local Church as ultimately responsible for the training and sending of Christian witnesses without the benefit of the methods and material resources of the West, this is the surer way to lay a foundation for the future. It makes more sense to begin with what the people know, with what they are familiar, and then move them slowly to higher levels of education according to their ability and maturity. Though there were only one or two government French language primary schools in the district, none of these new believers had attended these Western style educational institutions, nor did they know the French language. Therefore, it was more appropriate to go with the familiar, their own learning style.

In addition, let's not forget that the believers were just literate, as the result of the literacy program we initiated. This means that for the first time in the history of the tribe, they were learning by reading. Once having mastered the two basic Boko primers, it could take them another three to four months to increase their comprehension and retention rate from a few words, to a phrase, to a sentence and to larger blocks of information. While the Bokos may struggle with reading retention skills, in the West, we tend to struggle to memorize printed matter. If not, why the marketing of scores of books, tapes, CDs and seminars dealing with memorization? So these issues are not a matter of intelligence, but in part, of pedagogical expectancy.

In spite of this reading challenge, the discipling of these new believers was begun immediately. Though slow in the beginning, the comprehension of just one sentence and one truth at a time fit well into their high context learning style. Though this method seemingly teaches nothing in depth, what is learned is relevant to their present situation and applied immediately. They gained reading proficiency and learned the Word at the same time. It was exciting to see them painfully, but persistently make great strides of progress.

That is why it was imperative to adopt a biblically-sound and culturally-relevant pedagogy that matched their learning style for the discipling of new believers.

WHO?

Traditionally, the Boko society is patriarchal in that it is the older men who represent the authority structure in the family and in the village. Although older women have much to say about the outcome of some decisions and are the communicators of much of the tribal lore, it is the older men who bear the societal leadership responsibility.

In determining who would participate in this discipling process, several factors were taken under consideration.

Since it was the elders in this society that held the reins of leadership, wisdom and knowledge, it was decided that each village church elder would be invited to this program, regardless of their ability to read or lack thereof. We discovered that for some, their inability to learn to read was merely a matter of poor eyesight, not a lack of desire or ability.

This concurs with Paul's advice to the young churches that leaders are responsible "...for the equipping of the saints for the work of ministry, for the edifying of the body of Christ" (Eph. 4:11,12 NKJV). Timothy also was instructed that the teaching that he had learned from Paul was to be "...entrust to reliable men who will also be qualified to teach others" (2 Tim. 2:2).

With church leadership being the general standard for acceptance into this discipling program, the elders decided to invite the village church song leaders. These were men who not only led the worship services, but those gifted in composing the gospel words and music in the indigenous style. What a blessing this hymnology was, not only to worship services, but also in evangelism. Often those hearing the gospel for the first time would be hearing it in music familiar to their ears in the language that spoke to their hearts.

Finally, the elders wisely selected, with the approval of the congregation, other younger men spiritually attuned and gifted in reading skills, whom the elders would mentor as they all learned together.

The first group to come together numbered twelve from four villages. They were highly motivated to improve their reading skills as well as to learn the Word.

How?

CONTENT

The course work was not structured along the lines of a resident Bible School, such as a ten week course on the doctrine of God. But rather the teaching material was drawn from current problems, events and circumstances either personal or from the student's village church. This is not to say that doctrine was considered unimportant or disregarded. Although doctrine was not taught in depth, as in a fixed curriculum, it was taught in the context of the issues being studied. For example, when studying one of the Lord's miracles, the doctrine of God's omnipotence and His love were taken into account. (More detail on the course work will be presented in chapter seven.)

124

TEACHER

Who is the teacher? In the early stages of this program, the missionary, the only one who had had biblical training, was the teacher. However, as the disciples grew in their knowledge of the Word and matured in their daily walk with the Lord, the responsibility for teaching the group was intermittently delegated to the disciples.

The personal preparation of the teacher was foundational to comfortably handling the event-oriented system. Using the ten week syllabus approach, for example, the teacher would be in control of the direction of the study. Whereas, using the event-oriented approach, the teacher would be required to expound from the scripture on current topics brought up spontaneously by the students. The teacher's preparation, then, involved more heart preparation in the Word, the daily walk with the Lord and dependence on the Holy Spirit for moment by moment understanding and insight. This is one of the most difficult aspects of the event-oriented system for the expatriate teacher educated in the syllabus-oriented Western system. The feeling was that of having no control over the material, nor the direction it should take. And how will I ever be able to teach without prior preparation?

A sixfold commitment from the teacher is necessary to effectively disciple the students:

1) A vital, daily, living relationship with God the Father, through His Son, and walking in the power of the Holy Spirit.
2) A long term commitment to this ministry.

3) A passion to learn and understand the culture and language of the students.

4) The ability to communicate biblical truth in their language and in terms relevant to the local culture and learning styles.

5) The desire to develop a sensitivity to the student's personal needs, their level of spiritual maturity, Bible knowledge and literacy progress.

6) An acceptance of feeling 'out-of-control' or unprepared as a normal part of the event-oriented system where the expatriate teacher and student learn together.

STUDENTS

To qualify to enter the discipling program, the student candidate had to give witness to a growing relationship with God through Jesus Christ. This growth was to be fed by the student's commitment to a personal study of God's Word and prayer. His personal growth would be evidenced by how he handled his relationships, as well as his leadership responsibilities in his village church. All this being good, then there would be no problem meeting the next prerequisite of the approval of the elders and the congregation of his local church. Finally, the student must have completed the two Boko literacy primers, which would provide him a basis to continue gaining proficiency in his reading skills. Though not an absolute rule, this served as a general standard.

Exceptions were made for older leaders who had tried to learn to read, but because of bad eyesight or other valid reasons could not continue. These were included because of the insightful contributions they could make to the study groups based on their knowledge of the culture, their life's experiences and their relationship to Jesus.

With all of the above in place, the course content, the teacher and the qualified students, all that was needed was to decide when and where to meet.

WHEN?

Everyone of these men, married or not, was an integral part of an extended family household. They were subsistence farmers, responsible to contribute their fair share of physical labor to maintain the family farm. So as to minimize their time away from their farm and their church responsibilities, a monthly study cycle was arranged.

The cycle went like this. The teacher was to itinerate weekly to three different villages, spending one day in each village with the local students. This took place for the first three weeks of each month. Then the fourth week of the month, for two days, on Monday and Tuesday, all of the students came to a centrally located village.

The daily time frame for study generally ran from 9:00 a.m. to 5:00 p.m. with an hour break at noon. For the most part, this schedule met with the approval of the students' families, except when the farm work load was heavy (i.e. preparing new fields or at harvest time).

The students were very pleased that the missionary would actually come to their village once a week to sit all day with just three or four of them. From their perspective, to have a Westerner make this commitment made them feel significant and cared for. This was merely a demonstration of our oneness in Christ that, "There is neither Jew nor Greek, slave nor free, male nor female, for you are all one in Christ Jesus" (Gal. 3:28).

WHERE?

Would we meet in the village churches with the most mature elders? Or would we meet where the people were most zealous to share the gospel in unreached villages? In reality, at that time in the history of the Boko church there were not that many organized churches from which to choose. Three villages were chosen. There was Segbana, the first church among the Bokos, also the location of the missionary teacher. Next was Bobena, the second church historically. Then, Salonzi, the third church and perhaps the most zealous for the Lord. Of these, Bobena, being the more centrally located village, was selected to be the location of the monthly two day sessions.

As the number of churches, evangelists and elders increased in an area approximately 50 miles away from Segbana, it was necessary to establish a second study location. On their own initiative, they also appointed a leader from their discipleship group to be responsible for the training at this location. Interestingly, the church leadership had matured to the point that they took this action during the absence of a resident missionary.

The monthly study sessions were originally housed in the Bobena church building. Then sensing the need for a separate building, all of the Boko churches combined resources to erect a thatched adobe facility dedicated for the purpose of training church leadership.

Lodging for the students at their monthly two day sessions was provided by the members of the Bobena church, the students, of course, bringing their own bedding.

Each local church collected and sent to the Bobena church grain, yams and money to purchase meat and oil in proportion to the number of their own students in the program. Then, the Bobena church women formed a food committee to prepare the meals.

The investment made by the local churches in their men was more than rewarded as the students shared their increasing knowledge of God's truth in their home churches.

CHAPTER 7

EVENT-ORIENTED CLASSROOM PROCEDURE

THE WORD OF GOD: THE SOLE RESOURCE FOR TRUTH

The Boko sense of respect for authority and their belief in the power of one's word to either curse or bless, made it possible to establish a belief in and a respect for the power of the Word of God. The Bible teaches that the Word "…is living and active. Sharper than any double-edged sword, it penetrates even to dividing soul and spirit, joints and marrow: it judges the thoughts and attitudes of the heart" (Heb. 4:12). Having accepted this truth, it did not take much to teach them respect for the authority of the written Word as "…given by inspiration of God, and is profitable for doctrine, for reproof, for correction, for instruction in righteousness, that the man of God may be complete, thoroughly equipped for every good work" (2 Tim. 3:16 NKJV).

Foundational to the teaching was that God's Word was to be the judge of culture, not culture the judge of God's Word. This standard was for both the missionary's Western culture and the local culture. Appropriate proverbs and illustrative stories from the culture could be used in the study and in sermons as complementary to biblical truth. But inevitably the conclusions had to be backed up by the Word of God. Both missionary and student were rigidly held accountable to this principle and constantly reminded about it.

Cultural issues were freely discussed. However, conclusions were to be drawn or decisions made concerning cultural issues based on the truth of scripture. These conclusions/decisions were to be personalized either for individual believers or the body of believers and applied to their daily lives.

This concept was liberating both for student and teacher alike: the Word of God, the sole authority and resource for belief and behavior. Answers were to be researched and found in God's Word. In the case where there was disagreement, the argument was with God's Word, not man's (missionary's or national's) wisdom or desire. God's Word was the bottom line.

STUDY RESOURCES

Not having a syllabus focused on a given topic for a predetermined length of time, study subject matter came from a variety of sources.

STUDENTS' SUGGESTIONS

There were those times when a student would suggest a topic for study, for which the teacher would prepare material for a future session. For example, the question of dancing in the worship service came up. The teacher, in this case, myself, prepared an overview of dancing in the Bible. My conclusion was that dancing was used in worship in the Old Testament to glorify God, but that there was no mention of it in New Testament worship.

Before any conclusion could be drawn about dancing in church, questions about the significance of dancing and drumming in the Boko culture had to be asked.[1] Is there ever dancing just for fun? In what context is drumming and dancing used for spirit worship and why? Are there dances just for men or women? What are the implications when members of the opposite sex dance together? Their initial responses stimulated a series of thoughtful questions. After much discussion, they concluded that the dancing they had observed in the worship services seemed at that time to be more for the dancers to be seen by others, than to glorify God. They, therefore, decided dancing would not be allowed in the church, but that the drumming would be allowed to continue. However, drumming and dancing were then approved for church social events (i.e. baby dedications, weddings, etc.) The deciding issue here was, "Does the dancing in the worship service glorify God?"

At other times spontaneous questions arising out of the devotional given to start that very day were significant enough to be the basis of the day's study. For example, discussions arose at different times concerning traditional customs as related to: farming, hunting, childbirth, raising children, twins, weddings and funerals, etc. The direction of the discussion was up to the teacher's discretion, under the Holy Spirit's leadership, to make that decision while trusting Him for the biblical insight and illustrations to facilitate the teaching.

TEACHER'S SUGGESTIONS

A variety of topics, personal or church-wide, would arise during the teacher's interaction with the students or other believers. Then lessons addressing these topics would be prepared in advance for study. Some of the topics were:

- Taboo Issues
- The origin of animism (Gen. 3; Rom. 1:18-32)
- How to witness to animists (Gen. 1-3)
- How to witness to Muslims
- Cultural: female circumcision, spittle for healing, etc.
- Man-woman relationships
- Requests for insight into particular passages of scripture

SOME EXAMPLES:

Taboo issues have to do with what is forbidden by the culture. Taboos are conditional, resulting in negative consequences when transgressed. It would seem that every normal situation or activity in life from birth to death has its own set of taboos. These are instruments of control; spirit-beings over mankind. Control is maintained through the spirit-imposed element of the fear of the consequences for disobedience. The worst penalty for disobedience other than death would be mankind's loss of empowerment because of a broken relationship with the spirit world. In addition to that would be the specific punishment for the violation of the taboo. Take the case of preparing new farm land for planting yams; an arduous task. Family members and neighbors come together to help each other manually dig up and turn over the ground with short handled hoes. Depending on the size of the plot of ground selected, this work can take from five to ten days per farm. If at any time, a guinea fowl or small antelope should dart out of even the last square foot of ground to be turned over, that ground must be abandoned. It is taboo. Farming on that property is forbidden by the spirits. To plant yams there would be useless: a good crop of yams would not be harvested there. Out of fear of the retribution of the spirits, the farmers move to another site to begin the task all over again.

An important question for the discussion of this topic was, "What are the cultural implications for complying to the taboo?" In this case, the obvious answer would be, thanks to the spiritual powers, the family could expect a good yam harvest. For not complying, the family and the helping neighbors would reap the enmity of the spirits, the possibility of further retribution and certainly a poor harvest or no harvest at all.

Next the discussion would move to, "Does the Bible have anything to say about this?" Some missionaries would respond, "This is mere superstition, lies of Satan, ignorance; therefore, don't make an issue out of it." Others would say, "Yes, it is Satan's lie, but in reality, it is another of his plans designed to keep them in bondage and enslaved to the kingdom of darkness." While that is true, the animists need the assurance that because of their loving relationship with the all powerful Creator, they no longer need fear any of His creation, even a guinea fowl. Since their God is more powerful than created beings, He can be trusted to give them a good harvest in a 'taboo-designated' field.[2]

The final question would be, "What should believers do about this?" They responded, "Trust in the power and authority of God to protect them from the reprisals of the spirits, plant the yams in that field and believe that God will give a good harvest." In addition to this affirmation of their faith in God, this will also be an indisputable demonstration to unbelievers of the power of the true God.

Now as to a biblical study about man-woman relationships, this was initiated when I asked one of the elders if it would be appropriate to discuss an illicit relationship that had just come to my attention. One in the study group was having an affair with a married woman from another town. With this elder's approval, we then went together to the offender, himself married, to get his approval to discuss his situation. He freely consented. Remember, this is a society with little privacy, so everybody already knew about the affair.

This offender, Nikola, by name, had been one of a team of two sent by the church leaders[3] to an unreached village. At the request of the people of that village (who provided room and board), this team went for one month of evangelism, teaching Boko hymns and a literacy program.[4] Unfortunately, while there he became involved with a local married woman.

To provoke thinking and discussion, I started by saying that Satan motivates and controls people with fear. All agreed. Then, I dug myself deep into a hole by stating that God motivates His people by love, and since love is from God, and since Nikola (the offender) loves this woman and she loves him, this relationship must be all right. Sensing something amiss, but not knowing what it was, they, (to my dismay) reluctantly all agreed with my statement. As I recall, the Lord helped me out of this awkward situation by bringing to mind thirteen consecutive scripture references, one after the other with appropriate illustrations. It took a full day to put together God's plan for man's relationship with a woman. It was exciting for me to experience the Holy Spirit's guidance throughout this event-oriented study.

The application had yet to be made. So, I asked them if on the basis of God's Word this relationship would be approved by God? The response of all, including Nikola, was that he was acting contrary to God's Word and that he should end the relationship with this woman.

The next question the men asked was, "Will you, therefore, stop seeing her?" He said that it would be very difficult, but with our prayers and God's help he could.

For six months we all patiently prayed and counseled with him, but he never changed his way. With much pleading, then, the group implored him to leave her and live according to God's Word. Nikola, while acknowledging that what God had said in His Word was right, he, nevertheless, hardened his heart and said that he would not leave this woman. A silence of consternation and disbelief settled upon the hearts of these leaders. Reluctantly and with humility, they dismissed Nikola from the discipling group and his church leadership responsibilities, but said he could attend worship services. In due time, he disassociated himself from the church and moved sixty miles away with his two wives to learn how to make a living tailoring.

LOCAL CHURCH PROBLEMS

For the instruction of all, specific local church problems would be suggested for discussion, such as the incident when a couple was caught in the act of committing adultery in the church building. This had never happened before. What action should be taken? Should the couple be disciplined? If so, how and to what degree? What ought to be done at the church building, if anything?

The missionary teacher was away in ministry in another part of the country at this time, giving the church leaders a wonderful opportunity to trust the Holy Spirit alone for wisdom to resolve the problem. As always, the Lord was faithful. Interestingly, the pagan town elders showed their respect for a sacred place and disgust for the act committed there by sending the young lady away to her home village. The young man they sent to a neighboring village to make, by himself, 2000 mud blocks for a community project. The Christians were surprised and delighted because what they had envisioned for discipline was not nearly as severe. However, the church elders, after counsel, did dismiss the young man, a confessed believer, from the church with the hope that he would seek forgiveness and reconciliation.

As to the church building, the believers not knowing of any scriptural precedent, reacted culturally, yet, I believe, in a scripturally-appropriate manner under the guidance of the Holy

Spirit. Everyone knew that when this act is committed in a Muslim mosque, the door is closed and worship suspended until a goat is sacrificed and buried therein. The Christians decided to demonstrate their abhorrence of this sinful act in Jesus' House of Worship, by closing the doors of the church for worship until a cleansing ceremony could be held. The first act, a week later, was to whitewash the church, inside and out. The second act was to hold a worship service outside in front of the church at which they preached about the blood of Jesus shed for the cleansing of man's sin. This was followed with a communion service and a prayer, rededicating the church building back to the Lord to be used for His purposes. The door was then opened and all the people rushed in with much relief and rejoicing.

BIBLE STUDY METHOD

The memorization proficiency of these men was keen, though their reading retention capacity at this point was only one sentence at a time. This fact in itself dictated a very simple approach to studying the Bible . The narrative passages in the Gospels, particularly the Gospel of Mark, were effective in telling the life of Jesus and were a good place to start. In these stories, gospel truth, the power of Jesus and doctrine, could all be deducted from one brief scriptural account. The relevant truths then would be highlighted by a few brief questions.

Regardless of the topic or passage being discussed, three basic questions formed the pedagogical framework for all discussions. We found them to be culturally-relevant, biblically-appropriate and simple enough for a new literate or an advanced reader to use to teach others. Here are the three questions:

- **Cultural**: What are the cultural implications of this issue for a believer?
- **Biblical**: What does the Bible say about the issue?
- **Application**: What are you going to do about it?

This series of questions would be foundational to develop other appropriate questions about the issues. For example, under cultural, one could ask, "Is spirit worship involved in this issue?" and "How is the power of Jesus able to protect the Christian in this incident?", etc.

Or to obtain more biblical input, one could ask such questions as: Is there a command to follow? Is there a biblical principle to apply? Or to go even further, is this cultural issue in opposition to biblical teaching?

The cultural questions not only introduced the culture to the expatriate teacher, but also provoked the students to think about the implications of the cultural activities that they just normally react to without thinking. Scrutinizing his own culture in the light of biblical teaching also assisted in uncovering culturally-relevant practices that illustrate gospel truth. In the Boko concept of forgiveness, for example, to effect reconciliation of a broken relationship, the offender must go to the offended one with a mutual friend of theirs, a mediator. Because of the offense committed, the offender has no right to even be in the presence of the offended one. To have the audacity to do so would be interpreted in the culture as a mockery of the offended one, not an attempt at reconciliation. The offended one even had the right to attack the offender physically with impunity.

The culture, nevertheless, requires that the offended one must give the offender an audience, when he comes with a mediator. This mediator becomes the speaker assigned to recount the story of the wrongdoing. Then, as proof of his sincerity, the offender offers a gift to the offended one. This ceremony having been fulfilled, the offended one then is obliged by the culture, which established this practice, to forgive the offender.

After relating to the Bokos, line by line, that this also is the way God forgives us because of Jesus, our Mediator, who offered up the gift of His life to God for us, their response was, "Of course, if we do it this way, God must, too." If one persists, one can find many culturally-relevant practices that exemplify the truth of the gospel in terms of their understanding. The research is well worth the time and the effort just to see the light of God's truth dawn on their faces.

The final and indispensable element of the discipling sessions is prayer, which is like the golden thread that brings together the beauty and strength in a tapestry. Prayer is the key to enlightening the heart and applying truth to the believer's walk. Just as spending time and talking with someone personally is essential to a good relationship, so prayer is an expression of one's relationship with the Lord and an acknowledgment of His Lordship.

CHAPTER 7—NOTES:

1. One must understand just how important African drumming is in African culture. Dancing and rhythm are almost second nature to most Africans. So this was no small issue to resolve.

2. Some of the scriptures bearing on this point can be found in Appendix. B. Evil Forces and Power.

3. 'Church leaders' includes all those in the discipling group. They later became the Boko Church Council responsible to handle Boko church-wide problems and policy.

4. When a village requested teaching about the 'Jesus Way,' the church leaders sent a team to teach the gospel, Christian hymns and literacy, as well as determine the seriousness of the village people's intent to follow Jesus. Often their sincerity was demonstrated by the villagers' initiative to build their own meeting place called a 'Jesus House.'

CHAPTER 8

PROJECTED GOALS

1. Establish the Bible as the sole authority and standard for the believer's personal faith and behavior and for church-wide decisions.

2. Teach dependence on the Holy Spirit for wisdom, power and direction.

3. Teach independence from missionary paternalism.

4. Teach church leaders to assume the responsibility to make decisions as a body.

5. Teach a simple method of Bible study that is culturally transferable, yet simple enough to build into the church leadership confidence in their ability, under the Holy Spirit's guidance, to conduct leadership training sessions on their own.

6. Expect noticeable spiritual growth in the leadership.

7. Block the growth of legalism. Because animistic ritual must be performed in precisely the designated way to get favorable results from the spirits, this concept can, mistakenly, be carried over into their new faith. For example, during a worship service when I suggested prayer after two hymns, one of the elders said we could not pray yet because we had not yet sung the third hymn. In the early days, when I had been leading the services, I, apparently, usually led with three hymns and then had prayer. From their perception, I had set a pattern of 'ritual' that they believed had to be adhered to for the Lord's blessing.

8. Develop Boko church policy.

In summary, the Boko leadership is still in process and though four of the original group of twelve have left the Jesus Way, it is safe to say, that all of these goals have been attained to a greater or lesser degree in the lives of those who have kept the faith. It can also be said that many more have filled in the vacancies left by those four by responding to God's call on their lives to be messengers of the gospel of Jesus Christ to their own people and even into Nigeria.

It did not take long after my arrival in Africa to realize that the task of evangelizing and planting the church amongst the Boko people was colossal, even impossible, humanly speaking. During my times of weakness, God kept reassuring me that the gospel "…is the power of God for the salvation of everyone who believes" (Rom. 1:16) and that His Word "…will not return to me empty, but will accomplish what I desire and achieve

144

the purpose for which I sent it" (Isa. 55:11). He kept His word, for 'the gates of hell' in the animistic world continue to be broken down by the superior power of Jesus. The kingdom of God is being planted in many villages and in the hearts of many animistic people for all eternity. And now Great Commission believers are being trained and sent out by their own people to the unreached. These believers will be included with "every tribe and nation" that will be singing praises to the Lamb Of God in that wonderful home that God is preparing for His people. To God be the glory!

APPENDIX A

Dr. Steyne's Points of Contact With Animists [1]

1. God's Word
2. Supernatural Events
3. Disposed To Know Right And Wrong
4. Concept Of Power Encounter
5. Desire To Establish And Maintain Contact With The Spirit World
6. Desire For A Personal Relationship With A Spirit-being

APPENDIX B

Suggested Scripture For Study

- **Authority**: Matt. 28:18; Eph. 6:12; Col. 2:10,15; 1 Pet. 3:22.
- **Evil Forces**: John 12:31; John 14:30; 2 Cor. 4:4; Eph. 2:2,3; Eph. 6:12; Col. 1:13; 2 Tim. 2:26; Heb. 2:14,15; 1 John 5:19.
- **Power:** Luke 9:1; Luke 10:19; 1 Cor. 1:24; 1 Cor. 2:5; Eph. 1:19-21; Eph. 3:16,20; Col. 1:29; Col. 2:10; 1 Pet. 1:5; 2 Pet. 1:3.
- **Redemption**: Isa. 9:2; Matt. 4:16; Luke 4:18; John 12:31; John 14:30; John 17:15; Acts 14:15; Acts 26:18; 2 Cor. 4:5; Eph. 2:19; Col. 1:13; Col. 2:27; Heb. 2:14,15; 1 John 3:8.

APPENDIX C

Summary Of The Elements Of Paul's First Teachings To Thessalonian Animists[2]

(1) There is one living and true God (i.9).

(2) Idolatry is sinful and must be forsaken (i.9).

(3) The wrath of God is ready to be revealed against the heathen for their impurity (iv.6).

(4) The judgment will come suddenly and unexpectedly (v.2,3).

(5) Jesus the Son of God (i.10), given over to death (v.10), raised from the dead (v.14), is the Saviour from the wrath of God (i.10).

(6) The Kingdom of Jesus is now set up and all men are invited to enter it (ii.12).

(7) Those who believe and turn to God are now expecting the coming of the Saviour who will return from heaven to receive them (i.10; iv.15-17).

(8) Meanwhile their life must be pure (iv.1-8), useful (iv.11,12), and watchful (v.4-8).

(9) To that end God has given them His Holy Spirit (iv.8; v.19).

APPENDIX D

Characteristics Of Paul's Preaching [3]

(1) Conciliatoriness and sympathy with the condition of his hearers.

(2) Courage...in the direct assertion of unpalatable truth.

(3) Respect...St. Paul speaks to men as naturally religious persons, and appeals to them as living souls conscious of spiritual powers and spiritual needs.

(4) There is unhesitating confidence in the truth of his message and in its power to meet and satisfy the spiritual needs of men.

APPENDIX E

Some Biblical Facts About Man's Creation, Fall And Redemption:

- That man (man and woman) was created in the image of God: holy and with knowledge of life and moral discernment (Gen. 1:26,27; 2:15; Col. 3:10).
- That man was created to have a relationship with God (Gen. 1:26; 3:8,9).
- That man was created with the freedom of choice (Gen. 2:16,17).
- That man was given, by God, a position of supreme authority over all of creation (Gen. 1:26,28; 2:15,19,20; Ps. 8:5-8).
- That man was created with moral innocence (Gen. 2:25).
- That man was placed by God in a garden paradise in which to live forever (Gen. 1:29; 2:8-25: 3:22).
- That man lost it all by one act of disobedience (Gen. 3:23,24).
- Sin and death entered the world through one man...Adam (Rom. 5:12).
- Sin of one man was followed by condemnation and judgment (Rom. 5:16).
- God's grace gift of righteousness and eternal life came by one man, Jesus Christ (Rom 5:17).
- Through Jesus, man is reconciled to the Creator God (Rom. 5:10,11).

- Through Jesus blood, man is saved from God's wrath (Rom. 5:9).

APPENDIX F

Visual Aid Pictures

Picture One: Man With Power

Picture Two: Man Is Tempted

Picture Three: Man Obeys Satan, Rejects God

Picture Four: Consequences Of Rejecting God

Picture Five: Man Under Satan's Dominion

Picture Six: Gospel Messenger Arrives

Picture Seven: Christ's Power Is Greater Than Satan's

Picture Eight: Living Under Christ's Power

APPENDIX F NOTE:

Appendix F provides a set of eight visual aids with explanations in outline form (the presenter must fill in the details) to help the messenger present the gospel according to the concepts in this book.

Picture 1: Man With Power

- **CREATION STORY**
    - Light, lands, seas, plants, heavenly bodies, birds, animals, man and woman (Gen. 1:1-26).

- **GOD ESTABLISHES A RELATIONSHIP WITH MAN**
    - They are like each other (Gen. 1:27).
    - They have fellowship (Gen. 3:8).
    - Man is the crown of God's creation (Ps. 8:5).

- **GOD GAVE MAN AUTHORITY OVER ALL CREATION**
    - Childbirth (Gen. 1:28).
    - Animals and plant life (Gen. 1:26,28).
    - Animals named (2:19,20).

- **GOD ESTABLISHES A HAPPY MARRIAGE RELATIONSHIP**
    - Blessing of fruitfulness and increase (Gen. 1:28).
    - Companionship (Gen. 2:19).
    - Union of body and soul (Gen. 2:24).
    - Purity and trust (Gen. 2:25).

- **GOD PROVIDES A COMFORTABLE LIFE**
    - Tree of eternal life (Gen. 2:9; 3:22).
    - Food (Gen. 1:29,30; 2:9,16,17).
    - Garden location (Gen. 2:8,10,15).
    - Caretaker responsibility (Gen. 2:15).
    - Precious stones and metal (Gen. 2:12).
    - No death or sickness (Gen. 2:9; 3:23).
    - Freedom of choice (Gen. 3:16,17).

- **GOD CREATED MAN IN A STATE OF ALAFIA**

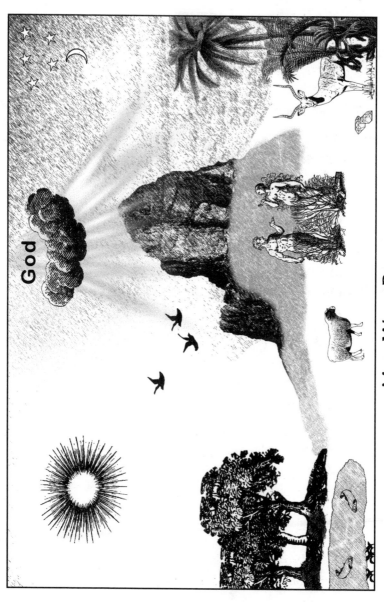

God

MAN WITH POWER

Picture 2:

Man Is Tempted

- **God declared one taboo (Gen. 2:16,17)**

- **Satan's deception**
    - Satan became a snake (Gen. 3:1).
    - His dialogue of doubts and half truths (Gen. 3:1-5).
      "You will not surely die" (Gen. 3:4).
    - Satan's lie, "You will be like God" (Gen. 3:5b).

- **Adam and Eve's self-centered humanity takes over (Isa. 53:6)**
    - Opportunity to be coequal with God.
    - Opportunity to control their own destiny.
    - Opportunity to exercise their ability to choose.

MAN IS TEMPTED

PICTURE 3:

MAN OBEYS SATAN, REJECTS GOD

- **ADAM AND EVE'S CHOICE: BELIEVE SATAN'S WORD, REJECT GOD'S (GEN. 3:6C)**
    - The fruit appealed to their senses: food and feeling (Gen. 3:6a).
    - The option to become wise appealed to their pride (Gen. 3:6b).

- **ADAM AND EVE'S REACTION**
    - Lost their innocence: clothed themselves (Gen. 3:7).
    - Guilt stricken: separated themselves from God (Gen. 3:8).
    - Refuse to accept responsibility for their choice (Gen. 3:12,13).

- **ADAM AND EVE EXCHANGED THE TRUTH OF GOD FOR A LIE (ROM. 1:21A, 25A)**

- **ADAM AND EVE LOST THEIR PERFECT ENVIRONMENT (GEN. 3:23,24)**

- **ADAM AND EVE LOST THEIR RELATIONSHIP WITH GOD: HIS ALAFIA, POWER AND LOVING PROVISION**

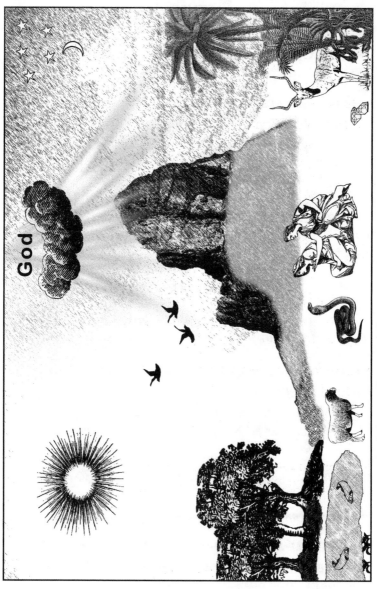

MAN OBEYS SATAN, REJECTS GOD

Picture 4:

Consequences Of Rejecting God

- **God cursed creation (Gen. 3:14-24)**
  - How did God curse creation?
    - ÷ Animals: domestic and wild, snakes (Gen. 3:14).
    - ÷ Women: childbirth; husband (Gen. 3:16).
    - ÷ Men: work; die (Gen. 3:19).
    - ÷ Ground: thorns and thistles (Gen. 3:17,18).
    - ÷ Life: death entered (Gen. 2:17,19; 3:22; Rom. 5:12).
    - ÷ Relationships flawed
      - Separation from God (Gen. 3:23,24; Isa. 59:2)
        - Satan (snake) prince of the power of the air (Eph. 2:2), Satan cuts off man's communication and fellowship with God.
      - Woman subject to man, no longer coequal (Gen. 3:16; 2:18).
    - ÷ Woman's child will crush Satan (Gen 3:15).
  - Why did God curse creation?
    - ÷ Man disobeyed and rejected God (Rom. 5:19).
    - ÷ Man obeyed Satan and became his slave (Rom. 6:16).

- **Animists worship a God-cursed creation (Rom. 1:25)**
  - Introduction of animistic belief and practice
  - See examples in chapter three.

- **Animists' minds and behavior became futile, foolish, impure, perverted and depraved (Rom. 1: 21, 22, 24, 26, 28)**

160

Picture 5: Man Under Satan's Dominion

- **Man's disobedience produced fear**
    - Man lost God's presence and security (Gen. 3:23,24).
    - Man lost the perfect environment (Gen. 3:23,24).
    - Man lost his power and authority over creation (Rom. 1:25).
    - Man entered Satan's kingdom of darkness (Rom. 1:21,22; Acts 26:18; Eph. 2:1,2; Col. 1:13; Gen. 3:22-24).
    - Man feared death (Heb. 2:15).

- **Man's disobedience produced enmity**
    - Enmity with God (Gen. 3:11-13; Eph 2:1,2; Col. 1:21).
    - Enmity between men (Gen. 4:8).
    - Enmity between man and animals; some became wild (Gen. 3:14).
    - Enmity between Satan and mankind (Gen. 3:15).

- **Man's disobedience produced perverted thinking**
    - Exchanged God's truth for a lie (Gen. 3:6; Rom. 1:25a).
    - Exchanged the worship of God to worship creation-like objects (Rom. 1:23).
    - Exchanged the worship of Creator to worship creation (Rom. 1:25b).

- **Man lost His perfect state of Alafia and power (Isa. 59:2)**

God

MAN UNDER SATAN'S DOMINION

Picture 6:

Gospel Messenger Arrives

- *MESSENGER LEARNS LANGUAGE AND CULTURE (1 COR. 9:20,21)*
- *MESSENGER COMMUNICATES THE GOSPEL OF JESUS' POWER*
    - Mark's Gospel (miracles of Jesus).
    - Jesus the power of God (Luke 9:1; 10:19; Col. 2:10; 1 Pet. 1:5).
    - Destroys the devil (Heb. 2:14, Gen 3:15).

- *MESSENGER COMMUNICATES ABOUT THE ANIMIST'S DILEMMA*
    - Daily struggle with evil spirits.
    - Animist's search for empowerment.
    - Man accepted Satan's word, rejected God's word.
    - God cursed creation.
    - Animists sacrifices to God-cursed creation; the Creator neglected.

- *MESSENGER COMMUNICATES THE GOSPEL OF RECONCILIATION*
    - Jesus died in man's place (Rom. 5:6,8).
    - Jesus saves man from God's wrath (Rom 5:9).
    - Jesus' death reconciles man and creation (Col. 1:20-22).
    - Satan's dominion ends at the cross (Col. 1:13).
    - Jesus' death provides forgiveness (Col. 1:14).
    - Believers will become members of God's family (Eph. 2:19).

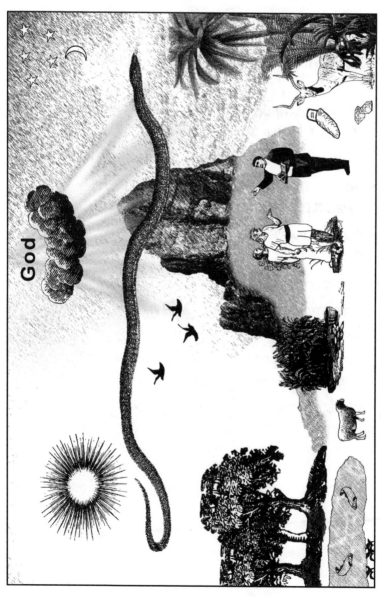

Picture 7:

Christ's Power Is Greater Than Satan's

- *Animist convinced of God's power to keep him safe (1 Pet. 1:5; Heb 2:15; 1 John 3:8)*

- *Satan's dominion ends (Gen. 3:15; Heb. 2:15)*

- *No fear of evil spirits (Col. 1:13; 2:10,15; 1 Pet. 3:21c,22)*

- *Animist makes a faith commitment to God, rejection of Satan (1 Thes. 1:9)*

- *Turns from the power of Satan to God (Acts 26:18)*

- *A relationship established with the Creator (John 1:12; Rom. 5:10,11; Eph. 2:19)*

- *Serves and worships the Creator (Eph. 2:10; Col. 3:16; 1 Thes. 1:9)*

- *Waits for the coming of God's Son (1 Thes. 1:10)*

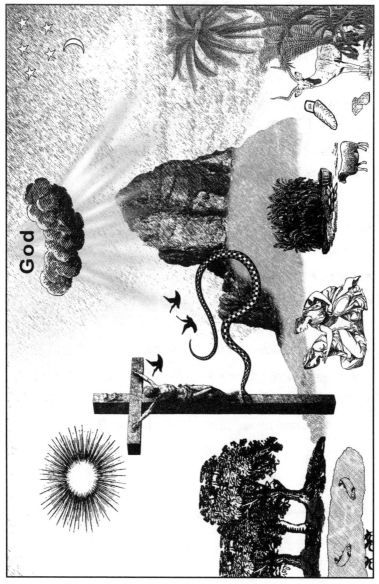

CHRIST'S POWER IS GREATER THAN SATAN'S

Picture 8:

Living Under Christ's Power

- *No fear of death: Satan stopped at the cross (Col. 2:15; Heb. 2:14,15)*

- *No fear of the curses: no barrier between God and man (Eph. 2:12-14a)*

- *No fear of God's wrath (Rom. 5:9)*

- *Believers have received forgiveness of sin (Acts 26:18; Col. 1:13,14; Heb. 9:28a)*

- *Believers have peace with God (Rom. 5:1; Col. 1:20)*

- *Believers empowered by God (Luke 9:1; 10:19; Eph. 1:19-21)*

- *Believers receive life/eternal life (1 John 5:11,12)*

- *Believers should live to please God (Col. 2:6,7; 1 Thess. 4:1,3-5)*

- *Jesus is Lord of all (Eph. 1:20,21; Col. 2:10)*

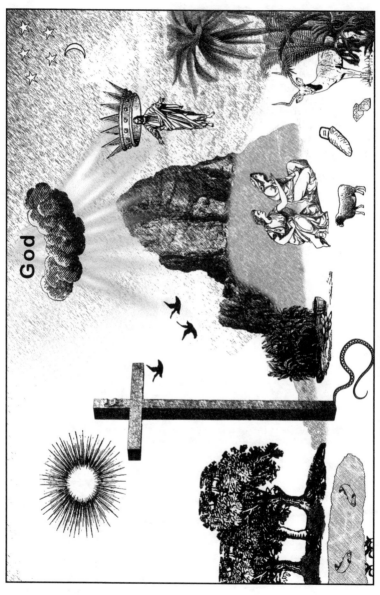

God

LIVING UNDER CHRIST'S POWER

APPENDIX—NOTES:

1. Steyne, Philip M., *God's of Power* (Columbia, SC: Impact International Foundation, 1990) pp. 207-212.

2. Allen, Roland, *Missionary Methods: St. Paul's Or Ours?* (London: World Dominion Press, 1956) pp. 90,91.
It is my observation that had missionaries studied and implemented Roland Allen's representation of St. Paul's methods, Church/Mission relationships would be healthier, more conciliatory and productive. It is not too late for present day missionaries to profit from Allen's timeless contributions to missiology.

3. Ibid., p. 85.

BIBLIOGRAPHY

Allen, Roland. *Missionary Methods: St. Paul's Or Ours*. London: World Dominion Press, 1953.

Augsburger, David W. *Pastoral Counseling Across Cultures*. Philadelphia: The Westminster Press, 1986.

Blue, Ken. *Authority To Heal*. Downers Grove, IL: InterVarsity Press, 1987.

Boulaga, F. Eboussi. *Christianity Without Fetishes*. Maryknoll, NY: Orbis Books, 1984.

Butler, Carolyn. "Applying God's Grace In An Animistic Society". *Evangelical Missions Quarterly*, Vol. 29, No. 4, (Wheaton: October 1993), pp. 384-385.

Conn, Harvie M. *Eternal Word and Changing Worlds: Theology, Anthropology and Mission in Trialogue*. Grand Rapids, MI: Academie Books, Zondervan, 1984.

Graham, Billy. *Angels: God's Secret Agents*. New York: Doubleday & Company, 1975.

Hall, Edward T. *Beyond Culture*. New York: Anchor Books, Doubleday, 1989.

Hay, Alex Rattray. *The New Testament Order For Church And Missionary*. Temperley, F.N.G.R., Argentina: New Testament Missionary Union, 1947.

Hesselgrave, David J. *Planting Churches Cross-Culturally: A Guide for Home and Foreign Missions*. Grand Rapids, MI: Baker Book House, 1980.

Hiebert, Paul G. *Cultural Anthropology*. Grand Rapids, MI: Baker Book House, 1983.

Hiebert, Paul G. *Anthropological Insights for Missionaries*. Grand Rapids, MI: Baker Book House, 1985.

Kraft, Charles H. and Tom N. Wisley, ed. *Readings in Dynamic Indigeneity*. Pasadena, CA: William Carey Library, 1979.

Laubach, Frank C. *How To Teach One and Win One For Christ*. Grand Rapids, MI: Zondervan Publishing Company, 1964.

Long, Meredith. "Perspectives On Christian Health Care". *CenterLine*. Vol.20, No.2. Billy Graham Center, Wheaton, IL: Spring/Summer, 1997.

Luzbetak, Louis J. *The Church and Cultures: An Applied Anthropology for the Religious Worker*. South Pasadena, CA: William Carey Library, 1975.

McIntyre, Loren. *The Incredible Incas and Their Timeless Land*. Washington, D.C.: National Geographic Society, 1988.

Metzger, Bruce M. *Lexical Aids For Students of New Testament Greek*. Princeton, NJ: Published by Author. Distributed by the Theological Book Agency, 1983.

Nida, Eugene A. *Message and Mission: The Communication of the Christian Faith*. New York: Harper and Row Publishers, 1960.

Nida, Eugene A. *Religion Across Cultures: A Study in the Communication of the Christian Faith*. Pasadena, CA: William Carey Library, 1968.

Parrinder, Geoffrey. *African Traditional Religion*. 3rd ed. London: Sheldon Press, 1974 (ATR).

Peterson, Eugene H. *The Message*. Colorado Springs, CO: NAVPRESS, 1995.

Richardson, Don. *Peace Child*. Glendale, California USA: G/L Regal Books, A Division of G/L Publications, 1974.

Smalley, William A. ed., *Readings in Missionary Anthropology*. Pasadena, CA: William Carey Library, 1978.

Steyne, Philip M. *Gods of Power*. Columbia, SC. Impact International Foundation, 1990.

James Chriselle."One People, One Earth". by Christele Jaime, *The Bolivian Times*. Thursday, February 10, 2000, Vol. VIII, No. 6, pp. 8,9.

"Potosi: The Mountain That Eats Men", *The Bolivian Times*. Thursday, January 6, 2000, Vol. VIII, No. 1. pp. 8,9 from *I Am Rich Potosi: The Mountain That Eats Men,* by Stephen Berry, Copyright 1999, The Monacelli Press.

The Holy Bible, New International Version. Copyright 1973, 1978, 1984 by International Bible Society.

The Holy Bible, The New King James Version. Copyright 1988 by Thomas Nelson.

Tippet, Alan. *Introduction to Missiology*. Pasadena, CA: William Carey Library, 1987.

Van Rheenen, Gailyn. *Communicating Christ in Animistic Contexts*. Grand Rapids, MI: Baker Book House, 1991.

Verkuyl, J. *Contemporary Missiology*. Grand Rapids, MI: William B. Erdmans Publishing Company, 1978.

Warneck, John. *The Living Christ and Dying Heathenism*. Grand Rapids, MI: Baker Book House, 1954.